Good Housekeeping
Grill It!

The Good Housekeeping Triple-Test Promise

We make sure that every recipe that bears the **Good Housekeeping** name works in any oven, with any brand of ingredient, no matter what. That's why, in our test kitchens at the **Good Housekeeping Research Institute**, we test each recipe at least three times—and, often, several more times after that.

When a recipe is first developed one member of our team prepares the dish and we judge it on these criteria: It must be **delicious, family-friendly, healthy,** and **easy to make.**

1. The recipe is then tested several times to fine-tune the flavor and ease of preparation, always by the same team member, using the same equipment.

2. Next, another team member follows the recipe as written, **varying the brands of ingredients and kinds of equipment.** Even the types of stoves we use are changed.

3. A third team member repeats the whole process **using yet another set of equipment and alternative ingredients.**

By the time our recipes appear on these pages, they are guaranteed to work in any kitchen, including yours. WE PROMISE.

Good Housekeeping

Grill It!

THE EDITORS OF
GOOD HOUSEKEEPING

HEARST BOOKS
A division of Sterling Publishing Co., Inc.

New York / London
www.sterlingpublishing.com

Rosemary Ellis
Editor in Chief

Susan Westmoreland
Food Director

Susan Deborah Goldsmith
Associate Food Director

Delia A. Hammock
Nutrition Director

Sharon Franke
Kitchen Appliances & Technology Director

Richard Eisenberg
Special Projects Director

Courtney Murphy
Design Director

Book Design by Renato Stanisic

Photography Credits

Front cover: Mary Ellen Bartley
Back cover (clockwise from top right): Alan
Richardson, Brian Hagiwara, Alan Richardson,
Brian Hagiwara
Spine: Mark Thomas

Alan Richardson: 21, 33, 51, 53, 61, 62, 69, 81,
83, 92, 119, 123, 147, 183, 193, 208, 211,
and 212 Ann Stratton: 17
Brian Hagiwara: 2, 26, 46, 65, 75, 89, 91, 99,
102, 107, 110, 113, 116, 124, 133, 139, 148,
151, 157, 168, 177, 180, 189, and 200
Brian Hagiwara, Alan Richardson, Mark
Thomas or Ann Stratton: 165, 173, and 205
Mark Thomas: 39, 134, and 186
Mary Ellen Bartley: 167

Library of Congress
Cataloging-in-Publication Data
Grill it! : Good housekeeping favorite recipes /
the editors of Good Housekeeping.
    p. cm. Includes index.
    ISBN 1-58816-446-2 1. Barbecue cookery.
I. Good housekeeping.
    TX840.B3G7475 2004
    641.5'784--dc22
                                    2004009408

10 9 8 7 6 5 4 3 2 1

Published by Hearst Books
A Division of Sterling Publishing Co., Inc.
387 Park Avenue South, New York, NY 10016

Good Housekeeping is a trademark owned by
Hearst Magazines Property, Inc., in USA,
and Hearst Communications, Inc., in Canada.
Hearst Books is a trademark owned by
Hearst Communications, Inc.

The Good Housekeeping Cookbook Seal
guarantees that the recipes in this cookbook
meet the strict standards of the Good
Housekeeping Research Institute, a source of
reliable information and a consumer advocate
since 1900. Every recipe has been triple-tested
for ease, reliability, and great taste.

www.goodhousekeeping.com

Distributed in Canada by Sterling Publishing
ᶜ/ₒ Canadian Manda Group,
165 Dufferin Street
Toronto, Ontario, Canada M6K 3H6

Distributed in Australia by Capricorn Link
(Australia) Pty. Ltd.
P.O. Box 704, Windsor, NSW 2756 Australia

Manufactured in China

ISBN 13: 978-1-58816-709-5
ISBN 10: 1-58816-709-7

CONTENTS

Grilled Basil Chicken
and Baby Greens

THE WAY TO GREAT GRILLING

Whether you cook over a shoebox-size hibachi or in a state-of-the-art gas-powered "kettle," you know that grilling imparts an incomparable flavor that no other cooking method can. The intense heat, the savory smoke, and the pleasure of cooking (and eating) outdoors all enhance the natural flavor of top-grade steaks, plump chicken breasts, sparkling seafood, and garden-fresh vegetables. You can even bake breads on the grill.

Before you light the fire, spend a few minutes with these pages to assess your grill and utensils, bone up on techniques and flavor-enhancing tricks, and review safety procedures.

Types of Grills

You can cook food over a wood fire built in an open pit, but most people appreciate the convenience of a modern barbecue grill. The most sophisticated grills allow you to adjust the heat by turning a knob, and even the most basic have adjustable racks so that you can place the food at the right distance from the fire.

Charcoal

Fueled by charcoal briquettes (pillow-shaped blocks made from hardwood charcoal) or natural hardwood charcoal chunks, these grills are relatively inexpensive. The simplest is the Japanese-style hibachi, a small cast-iron grill just right for a pocket-size patio. For more ambitious grilling, choose a large covered "kettle" with adjustable vents. In between is the versatile uncovered grill, sometimes called a brazier. Look for a charcoal grill made of heavy-gauge metal; the legs should be sturdy and positioned to keep the grill stable.

Gas
Today's popular gas grills, fueled by bottled propane or natural gas, can be as easy to light and control as your kitchen stove. They are available with a variety of options, including electric ignition, fuel gauge, extra burners (for simmering sauces or side dishes), warming racks, and storage cabinets. Some have porcelain-enameled cooking grids for easy cleaning. Gas grills may be grand enough to cook two dozen burgers at a time or to smoke a whole turkey. You don't sacrifice that delectable barbecue taste because the firebox of a gas grill contains ceramic "briquettes" or lava rocks (made of natural volcanic rock). Meat juices dripping onto these hot "coals" produce a savory flavor.

Electric
The latest thing in grilling is the electric barbecue. Like gas grills, most electric units have artificial briquettes for authentically smoky flavor; these may be removable, so you can also grill indoors, smoke-free. There are large electric grills to use in the backyard (within reach of a grounded electrical outlet) as well as tabletop models for small families and for all-weather indoor use.

Other Equipment
Cooking over hot coals calls for some specialized tools, and there are also optional gadgets to consider for easier grilling of fish, kabobs, etc. Here are the basics, plus some extras.

• **Grill topper** If you often grill delicate foods such as seafood and vegetables, you'll want a grill topper—a perforated metal sheet or mesh screen that provides a nearly smooth surface for grilling. Food is less likely to break up or fall through, and you can virtually "stir-fry" cut-up foods over the coals.

• **Grilling baskets** Another option for delicate or small foods; there are classic fish-shaped baskets (which hold whole fish) as well as square and oblong baskets with long handles to hold kabobs, baby vegetables, or fish fillets. Once the food is inside and the basket is clamped shut, you can turn the entire thing at once—easy!

• **Tongs** Better than a fork for turning foods, because they don't pierce the surface and release juices. Barbecue tongs should have heatproof handles and rounded ends that won't cut into the food.

• **Spatula** Use a long-handled one with a heatproof handle for flipping burgers and moving food around on a grill topper (see page 8).

• **Skewers** Long metal skewers are a must for kabobs. Choose skewers with flat shafts rather than round ones; food will be less likely to slip or turn as it cooks.

• **Basting brush** A heatproof handle and a long shaft are two definite brush requirements. Natural bristles will stand up to the heat better than synthetic ones.

• **Instant-read thermometer** This handy tool is about the size of a medical thermometer but made of metal. Insert it in food, and the dial at the top will give you a reading in seconds.

• **Grilling mitts** More serious versions of oven mitts, these are longer, to protect more of your arm, and better insulated, to protect you from higher heat. Heavy suede mitts are excellent.

• **Water spray bottle** The kind used to mist plants, adjusted so that it emits a narrow stream to quash flare-ups.

• **Brass-bristled scrub brush** Use this to clean the grill rack. It helps to remove the rack as soon as you've finished cooking, wrap it in dampened newspaper, and soak the whole thing with a hose. When you unwrap it, burned-on food will be softened. (Another time-saver: Line the firebox with heavy-duty foil before you grill.)

GRILLING PORK

CUT	COOK TO TEMPERATURE	APPROXIMATE COOKING TIME
Chops (rib or loin), 1" thick	160°F	12–14 minutes
Tenderloin, whole	160°F	15–25 minutes
Tenderloin steaks, 1/4" thick	160°F	6 minutes

For the Fire

Gas and electric grills are easy to light; just follow the manufacturer's directions. A charcoal fire requires a little more finesse. Be sure to leave enough time after starting the fire for the coals to burn down to gray ash before you start cooking. Allow 40 minutes to be on the safe side.

Getting Started

You don't want to run out of heat before the food is cooked, so start with enough briquettes. Estimate the right amount by spreading an even layer of briquettes over the bottom of the firebox. Before lighting, stack the briquettes into a pyramid to allow air to circulate among them. The following are options to help you get the fire going:

• **Chimney starter** An open-ended metal cylinder with a handle. Place crumpled newspaper in the bottom, top with briquettes, and light the paper through an opening in the bottom. The briquettes will quickly burn to ash-covered readiness.

• **Electric starter** A loop-shaped heating element with a handle, this device is placed in a bed of briquettes; plug it in, and the charcoal briquettes will ignite.

- **Self-starting briquettes** These are impregnated with starter fluid. A match will ignite them immediately. Don't add them to a fire that's already hot.

- **Liquid fire starter** Saturate briquettes with the liquid, then let stand for a minute before lighting. If you wait until the coals are ready for proper cooking (see "Fine-tuning" below), the fluid will have burned off and will not affect the flavor of the food. Never add liquid starter to a fire that's already burning, or to hot coals; a spark could ignite the whole can.

- **Solid fire starter** Place these waxy-looking cubes in the firebox, pile briquettes on top, and light. They're safer to handle than liquid starter.

Fine-tuning

You'll know the coals are ready when they are about 80 percent ashy gray (at night, you'll see them glow red). To test the heat, hold your palm above the coals at cooking height (about 6 inches): If the fire is low (above 200°F), you'll be able to keep your hand there for 5 to 6 seconds. If you can bear the heat for 4 to 5 seconds, the fire is moderate (above 300°F). If you can hold your palm over the fire for just 2 to 3 seconds, the fire is hot (above 375°F).

Tapping the coals will remove their ash cover and make the fire hotter. Pushing the coals together intensifies the heat, whereas spreading them apart decreases it. Opening the vents on a covered grill increases the temperature, and partially closing the vents lowers the heat.

Safety Tips

- Except for grills intended to be used indoors, always cook in the open air. You're safe under a shelter, such as a carport, or in the doorway (very close to the open door) of a garage, but never use a charcoal or gas grill in a closed building or room; the burning coals will consume the oxygen and fill the room with carbon monoxide, with possibly fatal results.

- Have a bucket of sand or water near the grill in case the fire gets out of hand.

- Never add liquid fire starter to an existing fire. The stream of fluid can ignite, and the can could explode.

• Keep an eye on the grill at all times, especially when children and/or pets are on the scene.

• Don't wear scarves or clothing with loose, billowy sleeves, or fringes, when cooking over coals.

• If the fire flares up or food catches fire, raise the rack and spread the coals apart. If necessary, squirt the fire with water from a spray bottle.

• If you want to coat the grill rack with nonstick cooking spray, do so while the rack is cool and at a good distance from the grill.

Marinades, Etc.

When food is to be cooked by intense dry heat—as in grilling—marinating and basting help keep it moist. Although the smoky taste of grilled food is naturally delicious, marinades and seasoning rubs (their dry counterparts) can add an extra dimension of flavor. Marinades often have an acidic component—vinegar, wine, yogurt—which penetrates the surface to a depth of 1/2 inch or so, thus tenderizing meat (if only slightly) and infusing it with flavor.

Here's the easiest way to marinate: Mix the marinade ingredients in a heavy-duty ziptight plastic bag, add the food, and seal the bag, pressing out most of the air. Put the bag on a platter to catch leaks or condensation. When marinating meat, poultry, and seafood for more than 30 minutes—or if it's a very warm day—place the bag in the refrigerator. Turn it occasionally to redistribute the marinade. If you're not using a plastic bag, place the food in a noncorrosive bowl or pan (glass, ceramic, stainless steel, or enamel) and cover it.

Delicate foods, such as seafood and boneless chicken breasts, can benefit from marinating just 15 minutes, and should not be left much longer (especially in an acid marinade) or they will begin to turn mushy. Large cuts of beef and pork, and substantial bone-in chicken parts should be marinated for at least an hour, but no more than 24 hours. A marinade can be brushed onto food as it grills, but since the liquid has been in contact with raw meat, it must be thoroughly cooked before you eat it. Stop basting 10 minutes before the food is done, or the marinade will not have sufficient time to cook. If you plan to serve a marinade as a sauce, you must boil it for at least 1 minute. Discard any leftover marinade; it cannot be reused.

Seasoning rubs are combinations of spices, dried herbs, salt, and, sometimes, moist ingredients such as mustard, oil, or pureed fresh herbs. The mixture is rubbed onto the food before grilling. If possible, apply the rub an hour or two in advance for maximum flavor. A seasoning rub can be used on its own, or complemented with a similarly seasoned sauce.

Basting sauces, including bottled barbecue sauce, should be thick enough to adhere to food as it cooks. Sweet sauces, made with liberal amounts of honey, molasses, or sugar, are likely to burn, so wait until the last 15 minutes of cooking time before brushing them on.

The Perfect Burger

• For juiciness and flavor, use relatively lean meat but not the very leanest. You need a little fat for great burgers.

• Don't overmix when combining meat and other ingredients, and don't squeeze or compress the mixture when shaping patties, or you'll end up with dry, tough burgers.

• To prevent sticking, get the grill good and hot before putting on the burgers.

GRILLING BEEF

CUT	COOK TO TEMPERATURE*	APPROXIMATE COOKING TIME
Steaks (porterhouse, T-bone, sirloin, rib-eye, top round):		
3/4" thick	145°F	6–8 minutes
1" thick	145°F	11–14 minutes
Steaks (flank or skirt)	145°F	15–20 minutes
Tenderloin, whole	135°F	30–40 minutes
Burgers, 1" thick	160°F	10–12 minutes

*For medium-rare

• Salt after cooking, not before; salt draws out juices.

• Never flatten or score burgers with a spatula as they cook, or you'll lose precious juices.

• For safety's sake, cook thoroughly, until just a trace of pink remains in the center (160°F). Burgers don't have to be well-done, but they should not be rare.

• Keep ground beef refrigerated up to 2 days in its supermarket wrap. For longer storage, rewrap in freezer wrap and freeze; use within 3 months.

Flavoring the Fire

In addition to seasoning the food you'll be grilling, you can also flavor the fire itself, or, more specifically, the smoke that rises from it. This works best in a covered grill, which holds in the smoke. Aromatic woods, such as mesquite or hickory, are well known for the tang they add to grilled meats. Herbs, spices, and other cooking ingredients add their own flavors.

Grilling woods are sold in chunks or chips to be tossed onto a charcoal fire or gas grill. You want the wood to smoke slowly, not burn quickly, so soak it in water before adding it to the coals. Chips require about half an hour of soaking; larger chunks should be soaked for up to two hours. Suit the wood to the food: Use oak and mesquite, which are strongly flavored, for cooking beef and pork; their smoke can overpower fish and poultry. Hickory's sweetness is well suited to turkey, chicken, and pork. Fruitwoods, such as apple and cherry, are mild enough to use with chicken and seafood. If using chunks of wood, add them to the fire from the start; place chips on the coals later in the cooking process.

Dried grapevines give off a subtle wine flavor, and corncobs (dried for a few days after you've cut off the kernels) produce a hickorylike smoke. Partially cracked nuts in the shell, soaked for 15 minutes or so, release their flavors when heated in the coals.

Whole spices and fresh or dried herbs can be placed on the fire to complement the seasonings in a marinade or rub. Soak them for about 30 minutes before using. Fennel is traditional for grilling fish, while rosemary, dill, thyme, bay leaves, and cilantro are other options. Experiment with other smoke flavorings, such as whole cinnamon sticks or cloves, strips of orange or lemon peel, and whole garlic cloves.

GRILLING POULTRY

CUT	COOK TO TEMPERATURE	APPROXIMATE COOKING TIME
Legs, bone-in	175°F	35–40 minutes
Thighs, bone-in	175°F	12–15 minutes
Thighs, boneless	175°F	10–12 minutes
Breasts, bone-in	175°F	30–35 minutes
Breasts, boneless	175°F	10–12 minutes
Cornish game hens, halved	175°F	35–45 minutes

Grilled Pitas with Caramelized Onions and Goat Cheese

APPETIZERS

Grilled Pizza

Quick-rise yeast gets mixed right in with the flour and salt and needs no proofing. Grilling pizza gives it a smoky flavor not unlike that from a wood-burning oven. If you like, grill onions, peppers, and sausages and let guests personalize their own pizzas.

PREP: 15 MINUTES PLUS DOUGH RESTING   GRILL: 5 TO 10 MINUTES
MAKES 12 APPETIZER SERVINGS

2 cups all-purpose flour
1 package quick-rise yeast
3/4 teaspoon salt
3/4 cup hot water (120° to 130°F)
2 teaspoons plus 2 tablespoons
    olive oil

8 ounces fresh mozzarella cheese,
    thinly sliced
12 fresh basil leaves
2 small ripe tomatoes, thinly sliced
salt
coarsely ground black pepper

1. Prepare outdoor grill for direct grilling over medium heat.
2. In large bowl, combine flour, yeast, and salt. Stir in hot water and 2 teaspoons oil until blended and dough comes away from side of bowl. Turn onto lightly floured surface; knead until smooth and elastic, about 5 minutes.
3. Shape dough into two 10-inch rounds or four 6-inch rounds (do not form rims). Cover with greased plastic wrap; let rest 15 minutes.
4. Place dough rounds on hot grill rack over medium heat and grill until underside of dough turns golden and grill marks appear, 2 to 5 minutes. With tongs, turn rounds over. Brush lightly with some remaining oil. Top with mozzarella, then basil and tomato slices. Grill until cheese begins to melt, 3 to 5 minutes longer. Drizzle with remaining olive oil and sprinkle with salt and pepper.

Each serving: About 170 calories, 7g protein, 17g carbohydrate, 8g total fat (3g saturated), 17mg cholesterol, 225mg sodium.

TIP: No time to make your own dough? Frozen bread dough from the supermarket or pizza dough purchased from your local pizza parlor is a great stand-in for homemade dough. Follow the thawing directions on the package if using frozen dough.

Grilled Flatbread

This is an excellent accompaniment to any grilled meat or as a base for delicious toppings like Flatbread with Salad (page 20) or Zahtar (page 23).

PREP: 15 MINUTES PLUS DOUGH RISING AND RESTING
GRILL: 4 TO 6 MINUTES EACH
MAKES 12 APPETIZER SERVINGS

1 package active dry yeast
1 teaspoon sugar
1 1/4 cups warm water (105° to 115°F)

about 4 cups all-purpose flour
about 3 tablespoons olive oil
2 teaspoons salt

1. In large bowl, combine yeast, sugar, and 1/4 cup warm water; stir to dissolve. Let stand until foamy, about 5 minutes.

2. With wooden spoon, stir in 1 1/2 cups flour, 2 tablespoons olive oil, salt, and remaining 1 cup warm water until combined. Gradually stir in 2 cups flour. With floured hand, knead mixture in bowl to combine.

3. Turn dough onto lightly floured surface and knead until smooth and elastic, about 10 minutes, working in more flour (about 1/2 cup), if necessary, to keep dough from sticking. Shape dough into ball and place in greased large bowl, turning dough to grease top. Cover bowl with plastic wrap and let rise in warm place (80° to 85°F) until doubled in volume, about 1 hour.

4. Punch down dough. Turn onto lightly floured surface; cover and let rest 15 minutes.

5. Grease two large cookie sheets. Shape dough into 4 balls. On lightly floured surface, with floured rolling pin, roll 1 ball at a time into a 12-inch round about 1/8-inch thick. Place rounds on prepared cookie sheets; lightly brush tops with some remaining oil.

6. Prepare outdoor grill for direct grilling over medium heat.

7. Place 1 round at a time, greased side down, on hot grill rack over medium heat and grill until grill marks appear on underside of dough and dough stiffens (dough may puff slightly), 2 to 3 minutes. Brush top with some remaining oil. With tongs, turn rounds over and grill until grill marks appear on underside and bread is cooked through, 2 to 3 minutes longer. Transfer flatbread to tray; keep warm. Repeat with remaining dough.

8. To serve, cut each flatbread into 6 wedges.

Each serving: About 200 calories, 5g protein, 33g carbohydrate, 5g total fat (1g saturated), 0mg cholesterol, 390mg sodium.

Flatbread with Salad

Try this salad "pizza" as an alternative to the usual tomato-and-cheese kind. The flatbread dough can be prepared up to 24 hours ahead. Prepare dough and rather than let it rise at room temperature, transfer it to a greased bowl, cover loosely with greased plastic wrap, and refrigerate up to 24 hours. Bring the dough to room temperature before proceeding with the recipe.

PREP: 20 MINUTES PLUS TIME TO PREPARE FLATBREAD
GRILL: 4 TO 6 MINUTES PER FLATBREAD
MAKES 8 APPETIZER SERVINGS

Grilled Flatbread (page 19)
2 tablespoons extravirgin olive oil
2 tablespoons red wine vinegar
1 teaspoon sugar
1 teaspoon Dijon mustard
1/4 teaspoon salt
1/8 teaspoon coarsely ground
  black pepper

6 cups salad greens, such as
  radicchio, endive, and arugula,
  cut into 1/2-inch pieces
2 ripe medium tomatoes, cut into
  1/2-inch pieces
1 small cucumber, peeled and cut
  into 1/2-inch pieces

1. Prepare Grilled Flatbread as directed through Step 5.
2. Prepare outdoor grill for direct grilling over medium heat.
3. About 10 minutes before grilling flatbread, prepare salad topping: In large bowl, with wire whisk, mix olive oil, vinegar, sugar, mustard, salt, and pepper until blended. Add salad greens, tomatoes, and cucumber to dressing in bowl; toss to coat well. Set aside.
4. Grill dough rounds as directed in Step 7 of flatbread recipe.
5. To serve, top each flatbread with about 2 cups salad. Cut each round into quarters. Serve 2 wedges per person.

Each serving: About 350 calories, 8g protein, 54g carbohydrate, 11g total fat (2g saturated), 0mg cholesterol, 680mg sodium.

Flatbread with Salad

Fired-Up Green-Onion Pancakes

These tempting appetizers are cooked right on the grill for a rustic look and great flavor. If you like, the dough can be prepared through Step 4 up to 24 hours ahead, covered loosely with greased plastic wrap, and refrigerated until you're ready to use it. When you're ready, proceed as directed.

PREP: 20 MINUTES PLUS DOUGH RISING
GRILL: 4 TO 6 MINUTES PER BATCH
MAKES 18 APPETIZER SERVINGS

1 1/4 cups warm water (105°
   to 115°F)
1 package active dry yeast
1 teaspoon sugar
about 4 1/4 cups all-purpose flour
12 green onions, chopped (about
   1 1/3 cups)

1 tablespoon olive oil
1 tablespoon Asian sesame oil
2 teaspoons salt
1 teaspoon coarsely ground
   black pepper

1. Prepare outdoor grill for direct grilling over medium heat.
2. In small bowl, combine warm water, yeast, and sugar; stir to dissolve. Let stand until foamy, about 5 minutes.
3. In large bowl, combine 1 1/2 cups flour, green onions, olive oil, sesame oil, salt, pepper, and yeast mixture. With wooden spoon, stir until blended. Gradually stir in 2 1/2 cups flour. With floured hand, knead mixture in bowl until combined.
4. Turn dough onto lightly floured surface and knead 10 minutes, until smooth and elastic, working in more flour (about 1/4 cup) if necessary.
5. Shape dough into ball; place in greased large bowl, turning dough to grease top. Cover bowl with plastic wrap and let stand in warm place (80° to 85°F) until doubled in volume, about 1 hour.
6. Punch down dough. Turn onto lightly floured surface; cover and let rest 15 minutes.
7. Shape dough into 6 balls. With hand, firmly press each ball into an 8-inch round. Place 3 rounds on hot grill rack over medium heat and grill until grill marks appear on underside and dough stiffens, 2 to 3 minutes. With tongs, turn rounds over and grill until grill marks appear on underside and pancakes are cooked through, 2 to 3 minutes longer. Repeat with remaining dough.

8. To serve, cut each pancake into 6 wedges

Each serving: About 130 calories, 4g protein, 25g carbohydrate, 2g total fat (0g saturated), 0mg cholesterol, 240mg sodium.

Flatbread with Zahtar

Top grilled flatbread with this popular Middle Eastern spread.

PREP: 30 MINUTES PLUS TIME TO PREPARE FLATBREAD
GRILL: 4 TO 6 MINUTES PER FLATBREAD
MAKES 12 APPETIZER SERVINGS

Grilled Flatbread (page 19)	2 teaspoons dried thyme
2 large lemons	1/2 teaspoon salt
1/2 cup sesame seeds, toasted	pinch ground red pepper (cayenne)
1/3 cup olive oil	1 garlic clove, crushed with garlic
3 tablespoons chopped fresh parsley	press

1. Prepare Grilled Flatbread as directed through Step 4.
2. While flatbreads are resting, prepare zahtar topping: From lemons, grate 1 tablespoon peel and squeeze 2 tablespoons juice. In small bowl, mix lemon juice and peel with remaining ingredients until combined. Set zahtar aside.
3. Roll dough as in Step 5 of flatbread recipe.
4. Prepare outdoor grill for direct grilling over medium heat.
5. Grill dough rounds as directed in Step 7 of flatbread recipe, except after turning each round over, do not brush with oil. With small metal spatula or spoon, spread scant 1/4 cup zahtar mixture on top of each flatbread. Grill until grill marks appear on underside and bread is cooked through, 2 to 3 minutes longer. Repeat with remaining dough and zahtar mixture.
6. To serve, cut each flatbread into 6 wedges.

Each serving: About 265 calories, 6g protein, 34g carbohydrate, 12g total fat (2g saturated), 0mg cholesterol, 445mg sodium.

Grilled Pitas with Caramelized Onions and Goat Cheese

Long, slow cooking makes onions especially sweet. The onions can be cooked up to three days in advance—just bring them to room temperature before spooning them over the goat-cheese topping.

PREP: 45 MINUTES   GRILL: 3 MINUTES
MAKES 8 APPETIZER SERVINGS

4 tablespoons olive oil
2 jumbo onions (1 pound each),
   coarsely chopped
1 teaspoon sugar
1/4 teaspoon salt
1/4 teaspoon dried tarragon

1/4 teaspoon dried thyme
4 (6-inch) pitas, cut
   horizontally in half
6 to 7 ounces soft goat cheese,
   crumbled
1 tablespoon chopped fresh parsley

1. In nonstick 12-inch skillet, heat 2 tablespoons oil over medium heat. Add onions, sugar, and salt. Cook, stirring frequently, until very soft, about 15 minutes. Reduce heat to medium-low and cook, stirring frequently, until onions are golden brown, about 20 minutes longer.
2. Prepare outdoor grill for direct grilling over low heat.
3. In cup, stir remaining 2 tablespoons oil, tarragon, and thyme. Brush cut sides of pitas with herb mixture. Spread with goat cheese, then top with caramelized onions.
4. Place pitas, topping side up, on grill rack over low heat, and grill until bottoms are crisp and topping is heated through, about 3 minutes.
5. To serve, sprinkle with parsley and cut each pita into 4 wedges.

Each serving: About 245 calories, 8g protein, 27g carbohydrate, 12g total fat (4g saturated), 10mg cholesterol, 310mg sodium.

TIP: For a tasty change, try this with whole-wheat pitas, crumbled feta cheese, and snipped dill.

Grilled Pitas with Caramelized Onions and Goat Cheese

Goat Cheese and Tomato Bruschetta
and Tuscan White-Bean Bruschetta

Goat Cheese and Tomato Bruschetta

You can make the goat-cheese mixture the day before, but bring it to room temperature before using, and assemble the bruschetta just before serving. For an even lovelier presentation, use a mix of red and yellow tomatoes and sprinkle with snipped chives.

PREP: 15 MINUTES   GRILL: 6 TO 10 MINUTES
MAKES 8 APPETIZER SERVINGS

1 loaf (8 ounces) Italian bread
1 package (5 1/2 ounces) soft mild
   goat cheese, such as Montrachet
1 teaspoon minced fresh oregano
1/4 teaspoon coarsely ground
   black pepper

2 ripe medium tomatoes, seeded
   and chopped
1/8 teaspoon salt
3 tablespoons olive oil
2 teaspoons minced fresh parsley
2 garlic cloves, each cut in half

1. Prepare outdoor grill for direct grilling over medium heat.

2. Cut off ends from loaf of bread; reserve for making bread crumbs. Cut loaf on diagonal into 1/2-inch-thick slices.

3. In small bowl, with fork, stir goat cheese, oregano, and pepper until blended. In medium bowl, stir tomatoes, salt, 1 tablespoon oil, and 1 teaspoon parsley.

4. Place bread slices on hot grill rack over medium heat and grill until lightly toasted, 3 to 5 minutes on each side. Rub 1 side of each toast slice with cut side of garlic. Brush with remaining 2 tablespoons oil.

5. Just before serving, spread goat-cheese mixture over garlic-rubbed side of toast and top with tomato mixture. Sprinkle with remaining parsley.

Each serving: About 180 calories, 6g protein, 16g carbohydrate, 10g total fat (4g saturated), 9mg cholesterol, 280mg sodium.

TIP: Want an even simpler preparation? Omit the goat-cheese mixture, add a tablespoon of chopped fresh basil to the tomatoes, and spoon the mixture over the grilled bread.

Tuscan White-Bean Bruschetta

A first course made with slices of grilled bread and the flavors of sunny Tuscany—the perfect way to begin an outdoor dinner cooked on the grill. For an attractive presentation, serve a tray of assorted bruschetta with a bowl of olives and extra olive oil for drizzling.

PREP: 15 MINUTES   GRILL: 6 TO 10 MINUTES
MAKES 8 APPETIZER SERVINGS

1 loaf (8 ounces) Italian bread
1 can (15 1/2 to 19 ounces) white
   kidney beans (cannellini), rinsed
   and drained
1 tablespoon fresh lemon juice
1 teaspoon minced fresh sage

1/4 teaspoon salt
1/8 teaspoon coarsely ground
   black pepper
3 tablespoons olive oil
3 teaspoons minced fresh parsley
2 garlic cloves, each cut in half

1. Prepare outdoor grill for direct grilling over medium heat.
2. Cut off ends from loaf of bread; reserve for making bread crumbs. Cut loaf on diagonal into 1/2-inch-thick slices.
3. In medium bowl, with fork, lightly mash beans with lemon juice, sage, salt, pepper, 1 tablespoon oil, and 2 teaspoons parsley.
4. Place bread slices on hot grill rack over medium heat and grill until lightly toasted, 3 to 5 minutes on each side. Rub 1 side of each toast slice with cut side of garlic. Brush with remaining 2 tablespoons olive oil.
5. Just before serving, spoon bean mixture over garlic-rubbed side of toast and sprinkle with remaining 1 teaspoon parsley.

Each serving: About 170 calories, 6g protein, 21g carbohydrate, 6g total fat (1g saturated), 0mg cholesterol, 315mg sodium.

TIP: To add extra flavor to the beans, use a fruity, full-bodied extravirgin olive oil.

Charbroiled Portobellos

If you can't find portobellos, substitute large cremini or white mushrooms. Steaming them first speeds up the grill time and requires less olive oil. Serve straight from the coals, or grill the mushrooms ahead and enjoy at room temperature.

PREP: 7 MINUTES PLUS MARINATING   COOK: 20 MINUTES
GRILL: 8 MINUTES   MAKES 8 APPETIZER SERVINGS

8 large portobello mushrooms (about 2 1/2 pounds), stems removed	1 teaspoon sugar
	1/2 teaspoon salt
1/4 cup olive oil	1/2 teaspoon dried rosemary
1/4 cup balsamic vinegar	1/4 teaspoon ground black pepper

1. Preheat oven to 400°F. Place rack in large roasting pan (17" by 11 1/2"). Pour in enough *boiling water* to cover bottom of pan without touching top of rack. Place mushrooms, stemmed side down, on rack; cover with foil and steam in oven 20 minutes.

2. Meanwhile, in large ziptight plastic bag, combine oil, vinegar, sugar, salt, rosemary, and pepper.

3. Remove mushrooms from roasting pan and pat dry with paper towels. Place mushrooms in bag with oil mixture, turning to coat. Seal bag, pressing out excess air. Place bag on plate; marinate 2 hours at room temperature, turning bag occasionally.

4. Meanwhile, prepare outdoor grill for direct grilling over medium heat.

5. Remove mushrooms from marinade; reserve marinade. Place mushrooms, stemmed side down, on grill rack over medium heat. Grill, turning once and basting frequently with marinade, until browned, about 8 minutes.

Each serving: About 90 calories, 2g protein, 6g carbohydrate, 7g total fat (1g saturated), 0mg cholesterol, 140mg sodium.

Portobello and Prosciutto Salad

Thick and meaty portobello mushrooms have a natural affinity for the grill. They're great in a salad or served alongside a thick, juicy steak. The stems, which are woody, may be saved and used in soups or stocks, where they'll lend an earthy flavor.

PREP: 30 MINUTES   GRILL: 8 TO 10 MINUTES
MAKES 4 APPETIZER SERVINGS

2 bunches arugula (about 8 ounces total), tough stems removed
2 tablespoons balsamic vinegar
2 tablespoons olive oil
2 tablespoons minced shallots
2 tablespoons chopped fresh parsley
1/4 teaspoon salt
1/4 teaspoon coarsely ground black pepper
4 portobello mushrooms (about 1 1/2 pounds), stems removed
8 ounces thinly sliced prosciutto
1/2 cup shaved Parmesan curls (1 ounce)

1. Prepare outdoor grill for direct grilling over medium heat. Arrange arugula on platter.
2. In small bowl, with wire whisk, mix vinegar, oil, shallots, parsley, salt, and pepper until blended.
3. Place mushrooms, stemmed side down, on hot grill rack over medium heat. Brush mushrooms with 1 tablespoon dressing. Grill 4 minutes. Turn mushrooms and brush with 2 tablespoons dressing. Grill until tender, about 5 minutes longer.
4. Thinly slice mushrooms and arrange on arugula. Spoon remaining dressing over salad. Arrange prosciutto on platter with salad. Top with Parmesan curls.

Each serving: About 270 calories, 23g protein, 9g carbohydrate, 17g total fat (4g saturated), 51mg cholesterol, 1,320mg sodium.

TIP: Grilled portobellos make great "pizzas." Once the mushrooms have been turned and grilled, top them with shredded mozzarella and continue grilling just until the cheese has melted. Top each with a sprinkling of finely chopped tomato and a sprig of fresh basil.

Grilled Buffalo Wings

Here's a real crowd-pleaser. We made the tangy blue-cheese dipping sauce with reduced-fat mayonnaise, cutting calories but not the great taste.

PREP: 20 MINUTES GRILL: 25 TO 27 MINUTES
MAKES 8 APPETIZER SERVINGS

BLUE-CHEESE DIPPING SAUCE
1 container (8 ounces) sour cream
  (about 3/4 cup)
4 ounces blue cheese, crumbled
  (about 1 cup)
3/4 cup reduced-fat mayonnaise
1 green onion, finely chopped
2 tablespoons cider vinegar
1 teaspoon Worcestershire sauce
1/4 teaspoon salt

BUFFALO WINGS
4 pounds medium chicken wings
  (about 24)
3/4 cup cayenne pepper sauce
celery and carrot sticks

1. Prepare dipping sauce: In small bowl, with wire whisk, mix sour cream, blue cheese, mayonnaise, green onion, vinegar, Worcestershire, and salt until well combined. Cover and refrigerate until ready to use or up to 3 days. Makes about 2 cups.

2. Prepare outdoor grill for covered direct grilling over medium heat.

3. Meanwhile, prepare wings: Separate wings at joints; refrigerate tips for another use. Place wings on hot rack over medium heat. Cover grill and cook wings, turning occasionally, until browned, about 20 minutes. Brush wings generously with some cayenne pepper sauce and grill, brushing with remaining sauce and turning frequently, until glazed and juices run clear when thickest part of wing is pierced with tip of knife, 5 to 7 minutes longer. Serve wings with dipping sauce and celery and carrot sticks.

Each serving wings: About 300 calories, 27g protein, 1g carbohydrate, 20g total fat (6g saturated), 86mg cholesterol, 675mg sodium.

Each tablespoon sauce: About 45 calories, 1g protein, 1g carbohydrate, 4g total fat (2g saturated), 8mg cholesterol, 105mg sodium.

TIP: Cayenne pepper sauce is a milder variety of hot pepper sauce that adds tang and flavor, not just heat. It can be found in the condiment section, near the ketchup, in the supermarket.

POULTRY

Stuffed Chicken Breasts with
Lemon and Basil Couscous

Grilled Whole Chicken with Lemon and Garlic

Use a covered grill to cook this deliciously seasoned chicken.

PREP: 15 MINUTES   GRILL: ABOUT 1 HOUR 15 MINUTES
MAKES 4 SERVINGS

1 whole chicken (about 3 1/2 pounds)	6 garlic cloves
1 lemon	1/2 teaspoon salt
1 small bunch thyme	1/4 teaspoon coarsely ground black pepper

1. Prepare charcoal grill for covered indirect-heat grilling with drip pan as manufacturer directs or preheat gas grill for covered indirect grilling over medium heat.

2. Remove giblets and neck from chicken; refrigerate for another use. Rinse chicken with cold running water; drain well; pat dry with paper towels.

3. From lemon, grate 2 teaspoons peel. Cut lemon into quarters and set aside. Chop enough thyme to equal 1 teaspoon; reserve remaining sprigs. Into cup, crush 2 garlic cloves with garlic press; reserve remaining 4 cloves. To garlic in cup, add lemon peel, chopped thyme, salt, and pepper; set aside. Place lemon quarters, whole garlic cloves, and 3 thyme sprigs inside cavity of chicken. Reserve remaining thyme sprigs for garnish if you like.

4. With chicken breast side up, lift wings up toward neck, then fold wing tips under back of chicken so wings stay in place. With string, loosely tie legs together. Rub lemon mixture on outside of chicken.

5. Place chicken on hot grill rack over medium heat. Cover grill and cook chicken until juices run clear when thickest part of chicken is pierced with tip of knife, about 1 hour and 15 minutes.

6. Place chicken on platter; let stand 10 minutes to set juices for easier carving. Garnish with thyme sprigs, if using. Remove skin from chicken before eating, if you like.

Each serving without skin: About 235 calories, 36g protein, 1g carbohydrate, 9g total fat (3g saturated), 109mg cholesterol, 395mg sodium.

All-American BBQ Chicken

Try our sweet and spicy sauce on pork spareribs, too. If you'd prefer, substitute chicken thighs or bone-in breasts for the whole chickens. Wait until the chicken has cooked for twenty minutes before brushing it with sauce, and it will become beautifully glazed without burning.

PREP: 1 HOUR   GRILL: 40 TO 45 MINUTES   MAKES 8 SERVINGS

2 tablespoons olive oil
1 large onion (12 ounces), chopped
2 cans (15 ounces each)
   tomato sauce
1 cup red wine vinegar
1/2 cup light (mild) molasses

1/4 cup Worcestershire sauce
1/3 cup packed brown sugar
3/4 teaspoon ground red pepper
   (cayenne)
2 whole chickens (3 1/2 pounds
   each), each cut into quarters

1. In 10-inch skillet, heat oil over medium heat. Add onion and cook until tender, about 10 minutes. Stir in tomato sauce, vinegar, molasses, Worcestershire, brown sugar, and ground red pepper; heat to boiling over high heat. Reduce heat to medium-low and cook, uncovered, until sauce thickens slightly, about 45 minutes. If not using sauce right away, cover and refrigerate to use within 2 weeks. Reserve 1 1/2 cups sauce to serve with chicken.

2. Meanwhile, prepare outdoor grill for direct grilling over medium heat.

3. Place chicken quarters on hot grill rack over medium heat and grill, turning once, 20 minutes. Generously brush chicken with some remaining barbecue sauce; grill, turning pieces often and brushing frequently with sauce, until juices run clear when thickest part of chicken is pierced with tip of knife, 20 to 25 minutes longer. Serve with reserved sauce.

Each serving: About 590 calories, 50g protein, 36g carbohydrate, 27g total fat (7g saturated), 154mg cholesterol, 880mg sodium.

TIP: For a lighter version, remove the skin from the chicken before grilling. Brush the grill with a little oil to prevent sticking and proceed with the recipe as directed.

Beer-Can Chicken

Your favorite brew keeps this chicken moist and juicy. If using a charcoal grill, you will need to add 10 fresh charcoal briquettes per side if more than 1 hour of cooking is required.

PREP: 15 MINUTES PLUS STANDING   GRILL: ABOUT 1 HOUR
MAKES 8 SERVINGS

3 tablespoons paprika
1 tablespoon sugar
1 tablespoon salt
2 teaspoons coarsely ground
   black pepper
1 teaspoon onion powder

1 teaspoon garlic powder
1 teaspoon ground red pepper
   (cayenne)
2 whole chickens (about
   3 1/2 pounds each)
2 cans (12 ounces each) beer

1. Prepare charcoal fire for covered indirect-heat grilling with drip pan as manufacturer directs or preheat gas grill for covered indirect grilling over medium heat.

2. In small bowl, combine paprika, sugar, salt, black pepper, onion powder, garlic powder, and ground red pepper.

3. Remove giblets and necks from chickens. Rinse chickens with cold running water and drain well; pat dry with paper towels. Sprinkle 1 tablespoon spice mixture inside cavity of each chicken. Rub remaining spice mixture all over chickens.

4. Wipe beer cans clean. Open beer cans; pour off $1/2$ cup beer from each can and reserve for another use. With can opener (church key), make four more holes in top of each can. With partially filled beer can on flat surface, hold 1 chicken upright, with opening of body cavity down, and slide chicken over top of beer can so can fits inside cavity. Repeat with remaining chicken and can. With large spatula, transfer chickens to center of hot grill rack over medium heat, keeping cans upright. (If using charcoal, place chickens over drip pan.) Spread out legs to balance chickens on rack.

5. Cover grill and cook chickens until juices run clear when thickest part of thigh is pierced with tip of knife, 1 hour to 1 hour 15 minutes.

6. With tongs and barbecue mitts, carefully remove chickens and cans from grill, being careful not to spill beer. Let chicken stand 10 minutes before lifting from cans. Transfer chickens to large platter or carving board; discard beer.

Each serving: About 350 calories, 39g protein, 4g carbohydrate, 19g total fat (5g saturated), 152mg cholesterol, 985mg sodium.

Grilled Basil Chicken and Baby Greens

Fragrant basil leaves turn everyday chicken breasts into something special. Slicing basil can be a breeze: Stack the leaves one on top of the other, then roll them up into a compact cylinder. Use a sharp knife to thinly slice the whole stack of leaves at once.

PREP: 20 MINUTES   GRILL: ABOUT 25 MINUTES   MAKES 4 SERVINGS

1 large bunch fresh basil
4 medium chicken breast halves
3/4 teaspoon salt
1/4 teaspoon coarsely ground
  black pepper
3 ripe medium tomatoes (1 pound),
  chopped

1/4 cup olive oil
2 tablespoons white wine vinegar
2 teaspoons freshly grated
  lemon peel
1/2 teaspoon Dijon mustard
4 ounces mixed baby greens (8 cups)
  or sliced romaine lettuce leaves

1. From bunch of basil, reserve 8 large leaves and measure 1 cup loosely packed small leaves. Finely slice enough of remaining leaves to equal 1/2 cup loosely packed. Cover and refrigerate small and sliced leaves.
2. Prepare outdoor grill for direct grilling over medium heat.
3. Place 2 reserved large basil leaves under skin of each chicken breast half. Sprinkle chicken breasts with 1/4 teaspoon salt and 1/8 teaspoon pepper. Place chicken, skin side up, on hot grill rack over medium heat. Grill chicken, turning once, until juices run clear when thickest part of breast is pierced with tip of knife and skin is brown and crisp, about 25 minutes.
4. Meanwhile, in small bowl, stir tomatoes, oil, vinegar, lemon peel, mustard, remaining 1/2 teaspoon salt, and remaining 1/8 teaspoon pepper.
5. To serve, in large bowl, toss baby greens with small basil leaves. Stir sliced basil leaves into tomato mixture. Toss greens with 1/2 cup tomato mixture. Divide greens among 4 dinner plates; top with chicken breasts. Spoon remaining tomato mixture over breasts.

Each serving: About 340 calories, 31g protein, 6g carbohydrate, 22g total fat (5g saturated), 83mg cholesterol, 490mg sodium.

Grilled Basil Chicken
and Baby Greens

Chicken with Gremolata Salsa

Gremolata, a sprightly combination of parsley, lemon peel, and garlic, is tossed with sun-ripened tomatoes for a full-flavored summer treat. For a change, try grated orange peel instead of the lemon, and basil instead of the parsley. If you like, remove the skin from the chicken and brush the quarters with 1 tablespoon of oil before cooking to lighten the dish.

PREP: 15 MINUTES   GRILL: 40 TO 45 MINUTES   MAKES 4 SERVINGS

4 ripe medium tomatoes, cut into
  1/4-inch pieces
2 tablespoons finely chopped
  fresh parsley
1 teaspoon freshly grated lemon peel
1 small garlic clove, minced

1 teaspoon olive oil
1 teaspoon salt
1/2 teaspoon coarsely ground
  black pepper
1 whole chicken (about 3 1/2
  pounds), cut into quarters

1. Prepare outdoor grill for direct grilling over medium heat.
2. In small bowl, stir tomatoes, parsley, lemon peel, garlic, oil, 1/2 teaspoon salt, and 1/4 teaspoon pepper; set salsa aside. Makes about 3 cups.
3. Sprinkle chicken with remaining 1/2 teaspoon salt and 1/4 teaspoon pepper.
4. Place chicken on hot grill rack over medium heat and grill 20 minutes. Turn chicken over and grill until juices run clear when thickest part of chicken is pierced with tip of knife, 20 to 25 minutes longer.
5. Serve chicken with salsa.

Each serving: About 460 calories, 49g protein, 6g carbohydrate, 25g total fat (7g saturated), 154mg cholesterol, 740mg sodium.

TIP Mix up a batch of the lemon-scented tomato salsa to spoon over grilled zucchini, eggplant, or a mixture of vegetables.

Chinese Five-Spice Grilled Chicken

Lots of flavor from just a few ingredients makes this a cinch for outdoor or indoor grilling.

PREP: 10 MINUTES PLUS MARINATING   GRILL: 24 TO 29 MINUTES
MAKES 4 SERVINGS

1/4 cup dry sherry
1 tablespoon Asian sesame oil
1 teaspoon Chinese five-spice powder
1/4 teaspoon ground red pepper
   (cayenne)

1 chicken (about 3 1/2 pounds), cut
   into 8 pieces and skin removed
   from all but wings, if you like
1/3 cup hoisin sauce
1 tablespoon soy sauce
1 teaspoon sesame seeds

1. In large bowl, stir sherry, sesame oil, five-spice powder, and ground red pepper until blended. Add chicken; toss until evenly coated. Cover bowl and let stand at room temperature, turning chicken occasionally, 15 minutes.
2. Prepare outdoor grill for covered direct grilling over medium heat.
3. Place chicken on hot grill rack over medium heat. Cover grill and cook, turning once and transferring pieces to platter as they are done, until juices run clear when thickest part of chicken is pierced with tip of knife, 20 to 25 minutes.
4. In small bowl, mix hoisin and soy sauces. Brush sauce all over chicken and return to grill. Cook, turning once, until glazed, 4 to 5 minutes longer.
5. To serve, place chicken on platter; sprinkle with sesame seeds.

Each serving without skin: About 350 calories, 41g protein, 10g carbohydrate, 15g total fat (4g saturated), 121mg cholesterol, 595mg sodium.

Grilled Chicken
Quarters, Your Way

Choose either a simple mix of herbs, white wine, and lemon juice modeled after a classic French tarragon roast chicken, or a more exotic blend of yogurt, garlic, and warm spices based on a northern Indian tradition.

PREP: 15 MINUTES PLUS MARINATING   GRILL: 20 TO 25 MINUTES
MAKES 4 SERVINGS

Indian Tandoori Marinade or French Tarragon Marinade (opposite)

1 whole chicken (about 3 1/2 pounds), cut into quarters, skin removed from all but wings

1. Prepare Indian Tandoori Marinade or French Tarragon Marinade as directed.

2. Pour marinade into large ziptight plastic bag; add chicken, turning to coat. Seal bag, pressing out excess air. Place bag on plate; let stand 15 minutes at room temperature or refrigerate 1 hour (or up to 24 hours), turning bag over occasionally.

3. Prepare outdoor grill for covered direct grilling over medium heat.

4. Remove chicken from bag; discard marinade. Place chicken on hot grill rack over medium heat. Cover grill and cook chicken, turning once and transferring pieces to platter as they are done, until juices run clear when thickest part of chicken is pierced with tip of knife, 20 to 25 minutes.

Indian Tandoori Marinade

In blender at medium speed, puree *1 (8-ounce) container plain low-fat yogurt*; *3 tablespoons coarsely chopped, peeled fresh ginger*; *2 tablespoons fresh lemon juice*; *1 tablespoon ground coriander*; *2 teaspoons ground cumin*; *1 teaspoon salt*; *$1/4$ teaspoon ground red pepper (cayenne)*; and *2 garlic cloves*, cut up, until smooth.

Each serving tandoori chicken: About 285 calories, 41g protein, 3g carbohydrate, 11g total fat (3g saturated), 123mg cholesterol, 430mg sodium.

French Tarragon Marinade

In small bowl, stir *2 small shallots, minced ($1/4$ cup)*; *1 cup dry white wine*; *2 tablespoons chopped fresh tarragon*; *1 teaspoon grated fresh lemon peel*; *$1/2$ teaspoon salt*; and *$1/4$ teaspoon coarsely ground black pepper* until mixed.

Each serving tarragon chicken: About 150 calories, 27g protein, 1g carbohydrate, 3g total fat (1g saturated), 72mg cholesterol, 210mg sodium.

Grilled Chicken Breasts, Three Ways

This simple recipe for grilled chicken breasts on the bone with crispy skin and juicy meat takes on a new dimension when one of our flavorful mixtures is rubbed under the skin: Sun-Dried Tomato and Basil, Garlic-Herb, or Sage-Butter.

PREP: 15 MINUTES   GRILL: ABOUT 25 MINUTES   MAKES 4 SERVINGS

**choice of seasoning mixture
  (opposite)**
**2 whole bone-in chicken breasts,
  split (about 2 1/2 pounds)**

1/2 teaspoon salt
**1/4 teaspoon coarsely ground
  black pepper**

1. Prepare outdoor grill for direct grilling over medium heat.

2. Prepare one seasoning mixture (see opposite) as directed.

3. With fingertips, separate skin from meat on each breast half. Rub equal amounts of seasoning mixture under skin of each breast. Sprinkle chicken with salt and pepper.

4. Place chicken on hot grill rack over medium heat and grill, turning over once, until juices run clear when thickest part of breast is pierced with tip of knife, about 25 minutes.

Sun-Dried Tomato and Basil Seasoning

In small bowl, mix *2 sun-dried tomatoes packed in seasoned olive oil*, minced, and *1/4 cup loosely packed fresh basil leaves*, finely chopped.

Each serving: About 305 calories, 46g protein, 0g carbohydrate, 12g total fat (3g saturated), 129mg cholesterol, 405mg sodium.

Garlic-Herb Seasoning

In small bowl, mix *2 garlic cloves*, crushed with garlic press; *1 tablespoon chopped fresh rosemary*; *1 tablespoon olive oil*; and *1 teaspoon freshly grated lemon peel.*

Each serving: About 335 calories, 46g protein, 1g carbohydrate, 15g total fat (4g saturated), 129mg cholesterol, 400mg sodium.

Sage-Butter Seasoning

In small bowl, mix *1 tablespoon butter or margarine*, softened, and *1 tablespoon chopped fresh sage leaves.*

Each serving: About 330 calories, 46g protein, 0g carbohydrate, 15g total fat (5g saturated), 137mg cholesterol, 417mg sodium.

Citrus-Sage Chicken

Citrus-Sage Chicken

You can double the citrus-sage mixture and reserve half of it. Serve the reserved mixture as a sauce to spoon over the grilled chicken. Fresh sage leaves have an earthy flavor. If you have extra citrus peels and sage and are using a charcoal grill, toss them onto the charcoal to flavor the smoke.

PREP: 25 MINUTES PLUS MARINATING   GRILL: 30 TO 35 MINUTES
MAKES 8 SERVINGS

2 large oranges
2 large lemons
1/4 cup chopped fresh sage
2 tablespoons olive oil
2 teaspoons salt

3/4 teaspoon coarsely ground
    black pepper
2 whole chickens (3 1/2 pounds
    each), each cut into eighths and
    skin removed

1. Grate 1 tablespoon peel and squeeze 3 tablespoons juice from oranges. Grate 1 tablespoon peel and squeeze 3 tablespoons juice from lemons.
2. In large bowl, with wire whisk or fork, combine orange and lemon peels, orange and lemon juices, sage, oil, salt, and pepper. Add chicken, turning to coat. Cover and refrigerate 2 hours, turning chicken pieces three or four times.
3. Prepare outdoor grill for direct grilling over medium heat.
4. Place chicken on hot grill rack over medium heat and grill 20 minutes. Turn chicken over and grill until juices run clear when chicken is pierced with tip of knife, 10 to 15 minutes longer.

Each serving: About 455 calories, 48g protein, 2g carbohydrate, 27g total fat (7g saturated), 154mg cholesterol, 725mg sodium.

TIP: Try this citrus, sage, and olive oil blend as a simple seasoning for veal chops or pork as well as for chicken.

Apricot-Ginger Chicken Legs

This quickly-put-together sauce can be served as a dipping sauce as well. If the sauce is too thick to spread, combine all the ingredients in a small saucepan and heat at the edge of the grill until the sauce is of spreading consistency. For a change of pace, substitute orange marmalade for the apricot preserves.

PREP: 10 MINUTES   GRILL: ABOUT 35 MINUTES   MAKES 6 SERVINGS

2 green onions, chopped
1/2 cup apricot preserves
1/3 cup ketchup
2 tablespoons cider vinegar
1 tablespoon plus 1 teaspoon grated, peeled fresh ginger

1 tablespoon plus 1 teaspoon soy sauce
6 large chicken legs (about 3 3/4 pounds)

1. Prepare outdoor grill for direct grilling over medium heat.
2. In small bowl, mix green onions, apricot preserves, ketchup, vinegar, ginger, and soy sauce.
3. Place chicken legs on hot grill rack over medium heat and grill until golden on both sides, about 10 minutes. Then, to avoid charring, stand chicken legs upright, leaning one against the other. Rearrange pieces from time to time and grill, brushing chicken legs frequently with apricot mixture during last 10 minutes of grilling, until fork-tender and juices run clear when pierced with knife, about 25 minutes longer.

Each serving: About 410 calories, 37g protein, 22g carbohydrate, 19g total fat (5g saturated), 129mg cholesterol, 520mg sodium.

TIP: If you prefer a smooth sauce, start with 3/4 cup of apricot preserves and push it through a fine-mesh sieve to remove large chunks.

Flame-Cooked Chicken Saltimbocca

So simple, yet so flavorful, this dish will quickly become a part of your outdoor repertoire. Remember, cutlets are thin, so make sure you don't overcook them. These would be delicious served between two layers of grilled focaccia or our Grilled Flatbread (page 19).

PREP: 15 MINUTES   GRILL: 8 MINUTES   MAKES 8 SERVINGS

2 tablespoons fresh lemon juice
1 tablespoon olive oil
8 chicken cutlets or skinless,
   boneless chicken breast halves
   with tenderloins removed
   (2 pounds)

24 large fresh sage leaves
8 thin slices prosciutto (4 ounces)

1. Prepare outdoor grill for direct grilling over medium heat.
2. In large bowl, with fork, mix lemon juice and olive oil. Add chicken and toss to coat.
3. Place 3 sage leaves on each cutlet or breast half, then wrap each with 1 slice prosciutto. Place chicken on hot grill rack over medium heat and grill, turning once, until juices run clear when thickest part of breast is pierced with tip of knife, 8 minutes.

Each serving: About 195 calories, 31g protein, 1g carbohydrate, 7g total fat (2g saturated), 83mg cholesterol, 410mg sodium.

TIP: If you can't find prosciutto, substitute slices of lean bacon or Canadian bacon.

BBQ for a Crowd

To help you enjoy more time with your guests, completely precook the chicken in the oven and keep it refrigerated up to a day. Then, when you're ready to dine, all you have to do is warm up the chicken on the grill and brush on our delicious barbecue sauce.

PREP: 30 MINUTES   BAKE: 1 HOUR   GRILL: ABOUT 20 MINUTES
MAKES 10 SERVINGS

10 pounds bone-in chicken parts, skin removed, if you like
1 tablespoon olive oil
1 jumbo onion (1 pound), chopped
1 tablespoon grated, peeled fresh ginger
3 garlic cloves, crushed with garlic press
1/4 cup chili powder

1 can (28 ounces) whole tomatoes in puree
1/2 cup cider vinegar
1/4 cup packed dark brown sugar
1/4 cup light (mild) molasses
3 tablespoons Dijon mustard
2 tablespoons Worcestershire sauce
1 teaspoon salt

1. Preheat oven to 425°F. Place chicken pieces in large roasting pan (17" by 11 1/2"); cover tightly with foil. Bake until juices run clear when thickest part of chicken is pierced with tip of knife, about 1 hour. Transfer chicken to large platter; cover and refrigerate until ready to grill.

2. Meanwhile, in 5- to 6-quart saucepot, heat oil over medium heat until hot. (Do not use smaller pan; sauce bubbles up and splatters during cooking—the deeper the pan, the better.) Add onion and ginger; cook, stirring occasionally, until onion is tender and golden, about 10 minutes. Add garlic and chili powder; cook, stirring, 1 minute longer. Remove saucepot from heat; stir in tomatoes with their puree, vinegar, brown sugar, molasses, mustard, Worcestershire, and salt.

3. Spoon about one-third of sauce into blender. At low speed, puree sauce until smooth; pour sauce into bowl. Repeat with remaining sauce. Return sauce to saucepot; heat to boiling over high heat. Reduce heat to medium, and cook, partially covered, 1 minute, stirring occasionally. Cover and refrigerate sauce if not using right away. Sauce will keep up to 1 week in refrigerator or up to 2 months in freezer. Makes about 4 1/2 cups.

4. Prepare outdoor grill for direct grilling over medium heat.

5. Place chicken on hot grill rack over medium heat and grill, turning once, 10 minutes. Brush barbecue sauce over chicken and grill, turning chicken pieces and brushing with barbecue sauce, until sauce is hot and bubbly and chicken is heated through, about 10 minutes longer.

Each serving without skin: About 360 calories, 41g protein, 21g carbohydrate, 13g total fat (3g saturated), 121mg cholesterol, 645mg sodium.

BBQ for a Crowd

Polynesian Drumsticks

A quick marinade adds a sweet and tangy glaze to grilled skinless drumsticks—a favorite with everyone in the family.

PREP: 15 MINUTES PLUS MARINATING   GRILL: 25 MINUTES
MAKES 4 SERVINGS

1 can (8 ounces) crushed pineapple
  in unsweetened pineapple juice
1/4 cup packed brown sugar
3 tablespoons soy sauce
1 tablespoon grated, peeled fresh
  ginger

1 garlic clove, crushed with
  garlic press
12 chicken drumsticks (about
  4 pounds), skin removed

1. In blender, puree crushed pineapple with its juice, brown sugar, soy sauce, ginger, and garlic until smooth. Spoon $1/2$ cup pineapple puree into large zip-tight bag; reserve remaining puree for grilling. Add drumsticks to bag, turning to coat. Let stand at room temperature 15 minutes.

2. Prepare outdoor grill for direct grilling over medium heat.

3. Remove drumsticks from bag; discard bag with marinade. Place the drumsticks on hot grill rack over medium heat and grill, turning once, 15 minutes. Grill, brushing twice with reserved pineapple puree and turning occasionally, until drumsticks are golden and juices run clear when thickest part of chicken is pierced with tip of knife, 10 to 15 minutes longer.

Each serving: About 260 calories, 38g protein, 8g carbohydrate, 8g total fat (2g saturated), 123mg cholesterol, 385mg sodium.

Polynesian Drumsticks

Chicken Grilled in Foil Packet

We took three of our favorite chicken recipes usually prepared in a skillet and adapted them to the summer grill. Look for foil cooking bags in your supermarket where foil and plastic wrap are sold. If you can't find them, you can make your own: Layer two 24" by 18" sheets heavy-duty foil to make a double thickness. Place recipe ingredients in center of foil. Bring short ends of foil up and over ingredients and fold over two to three times to seal well. Fold over remaining sides of foil two to three times to seal in juices.

PREP: 15 MINUTES   GRILL: 15 MINUTES PLUS STANDING
MAKES 4 SERVINGS

- 4 medium skinless, boneless chicken breast halves (about 1 1/4 pounds)
- 3 tablespoons drained capers, chopped
- 2 tablespoons butter or margarine, cut into pieces
- 1/4 teaspoon coarsely ground black pepper
- 1/4 cup loosely packed parsley leaves, chopped
- 2 teaspoons cornstarch
- 1 tablespoon water

1. Prepare outdoor grill for direct grilling over medium heat.
2. Place chicken, capers, butter, pepper, and 2 tablespoons parsley in 17" by 15" extra-heavy-duty foil cooking bag. In cup, stir cornstarch with water. Add cornstarch mixture to bag and fold to seal as label directs. Shake bag gently to combine ingredients.
3. Place foil packet on hot grill rack over medium heat and cook chicken, turning packet over once halfway through cooking, 15 minutes. Remove packet from grill; let stand 5 minutes.
4. Before serving, with kitchen shears, cut an X in top of foil packet to let steam escape. Open packet and check to make sure that juices run clear when thickest part of chicken breast is pierced with tip of knife. Sprinkle chicken with remaining parsley.

Each serving: About 215 calories, 33g protein, 2g carbohydrate, 8g total fat (5g saturated), 98mg cholesterol, 342mg sodium.

Mushroom and Marsala Chicken

Prepare Chicken Grilled in Foil Packet as directed, but omit capers in Step 2 and add *8 ounces sliced mushrooms, 2 tablespoons dry or sweet marsala wine, 1/2 teaspoon salt,* and *1 garlic clove,* crushed with garlic press, to packet before grilling. In Step 4, sprinkle with an additional *1 tablespoon marsala wine* before serving.

Each serving: About 230 calories, 34g protein, 4g carbohydrate, 8g total fat (5g saturated), 98mg cholesterol, 632mg sodium.

Buffalo-Style Chicken

Prepare Chicken Grilled in Foil Packet as directed, but omit capers in Step 2 and add *3 tablespoons cayenne pepper sauce* to packet before grilling. Serve chicken with *3 medium carrots,* peeled and cut into 3-inch-long sticks, *3 celery stalks,* cut into 3-inch-long sticks, and *1/4 cup crumbled blue cheese (1 ounce).*

Each serving: About 265 calories, 35g protein, 8g carbohydrate, 10g total fat (6g saturated), 104mg cholesterol, 882mg sodium.

Stuffed Chicken Breasts with Lemon and Basil Couscous

Garlic-and-herb cheese and roasted peppers are the surprise filling for these boneless breasts. Accompanied by a lemony herb couscous, this dish is elegant enough for guests but easy enough for a weeknight family dinner.

PREP: 20 MINUTES   GRILL: 12 TO 15 MINUTES   MAKES 4 SERVINGS

CHICKEN BREASTS

- 4 medium skinless, boneless chicken breast halves (about 1 1/4 pounds)
- 1/4 cup light garlic-and-herb spreadable cheese (about half 4.4-ounce package)
- 1/4 cup drained and chopped jarred roasted red peppers
- 8 whole fresh basil leaves, chopped
- 1 teaspoon extravirgin olive oil
- 1/2 teaspoon salt
- 1/4 teaspoon coarsely ground black pepper

COUSCOUS

- 1 tablespoon extravirgin olive oil
- 1/2 teaspoon salt
- 1/4 teaspoon coarsely ground black pepper
- 1 1/3 cups water
- 1 cup couscous
- 1 cup loosely packed fresh basil leaves, coarsely chopped
- 2 tablespoons fresh lemon juice

1. Prepare chicken breasts: With tip of knife, cut each chicken breast along one long side, keeping knife parallel to surface of breast, to form a deep pocket with as small an opening as possible.

2. Prepare outdoor grill for direct grilling over medium heat.

3. In small bowl, combine cheese, peppers, and basil. Stuff one-fourth cheese mixture into each chicken pocket. Rub oil on outside of chicken and sprinkle with salt and pepper.

4. Prepare couscous: In 2-quart saucepan, heat oil, salt, pepper, and water to boiling over high heat; stir in couscous. Cover pan; remove from heat and let stand at least 5 minutes.

5. Meanwhile, place chicken on hot grill rack over medium heat and grill, turning once, until juices run clear when thickest part of breast is pierced with tip of knife, 12 to 15 minutes.

6. To serve, add basil and lemon juice to couscous; fluff with fork until well mixed. Spoon couscous onto 4 dinner plates; top with chicken breasts.

Each serving chicken: About 255 calories, 35g protein, 4g carbohydrate, 10g total fat (5g saturated), 113mg cholesterol, 560mg sodium.

Each serving couscous: About 205 calories, 6g protein, 37g carbohydrate, 4g total fat (1g saturated), 0mg cholesterol, 295mg sodium.

Stuffed Chicken Breasts with Lemon and Basil Couscous

Grilled Chicken with Baby Spinach and Nectarines

Prepare this colorful salad with any ripe summer fruit. Try substituting a soft, creamy goat cheese for the feta and add a topping of chopped toasted pecans for extra crunch.

PREP: 25 MINUTES   GRILL: ABOUT 14 MINUTES   MAKES 4 SERVINGS

4 small skinless, boneless chicken breast halves (about 1 pound)
1 teaspoon fresh thyme
3/4 teaspoon salt
1/2 teaspoon coarsely ground black pepper
2 tablespoons olive oil
1 tablespoon balsamic vinegar
1/2 teaspoon Dijon mustard

1 shallot, minced
2 large ripe nectarines, pitted and sliced
1/2 English (seedless) cucumber, cut lengthwise in half, then thinly sliced crosswise
8 ounces baby spinach
2 ounces feta cheese, crumbled

1. Prepare outdoor grill for direct grilling over medium heat.
2. Rub chicken with thyme, 1/2 teaspoon salt, and 1/4 teaspoon pepper. Place chicken on hot grill rack over medium heat and grill, turning once, until juices run clear when thickest part of breast is pierced with tip of knife, about 7 minutes per side. Transfer chicken to cutting board; set aside until cool enough to handle.
3. Meanwhile, in large bowl, with wire whisk, mix olive oil, vinegar, mustard, shallot, remaining 1/4 teaspoon salt, and the remaining 1/4 teaspoon pepper. Stir in nectarines and cucumber.
4. To serve, cut chicken into 1/2-inch-thick slices. Toss spinach with nectarine mixture. Divide salad among 4 plates; top with sliced chicken and feta.

Each serving: About 290 calories, 31g protein, 15g carbohydrate, 12g total fat (3g saturated), 78mg cholesterol, 730mg sodium.

TIP: Baby spinach, with its soft, delicate leaves, is often sold in prepackaged bags. If you can't find baby spinach, look for spinach with smooth, rather than ruffled, leaves and tender stems. Or substitute a mix of baby greens.

Chicken Parmesan

This grilled version of an old favorite still has a layer of mozzarella cheese and a sprinkling of Parmesan, but we've replaced the usual tomato sauce with juicy slices of tomato and fresh basil leaves.

Prep: 10 minutes   Grill: 8 to 10 minutes   Makes 4 servings

4 medium skinless, boneless chicken breast halves (about 1 1/4 pounds)

2 teaspoons olive oil

1/2 teaspoon salt

1/4 teaspoon coarsely ground black pepper

4 ounces part-skim mozzarella cheese, cut into 1/4-inch-thick slices and each slice cut crosswise in half

2 medium tomatoes, cut into 1/4-inch-thick slices

1/4 cup freshly grated Parmesan cheese

3/4 cup loosely packed fresh basil leaves

1. Prepare outdoor grill for direct grilling over medium heat.
2. If necessary, pound chicken breasts to uniform 1/4-inch thickness. Coat chicken with oil and sprinkle with salt and pepper.
3. Place chicken on hot grill rack over medium-high heat and grill 4 minutes. Turn chicken and top with mozzarella, tomatoes, and Parmesan. Cook until juices run clear when chicken is pierced with tip of knife, 4 to 6 minutes longer. Transfer chicken to platter and top with basil leaves.

Each serving: About 340 calories, 49g protein, 4g carbohydrate, 13g total fat (5g saturated), 129mg cholesterol, 615mg sodium.

Jerk Chicken Kabobs

The classic Jamaican seasoning called jerk is a zesty blend of herbs and spices that packs a wallop of flavor.

PREP: 40 MINUTES   GRILL: 10 TO 12 MINUTES   MAKES 4 SERVINGS

5 large green onions
1 jalapeño chile, seeded and chopped
1-inch piece fresh ginger, peeled and
   chopped
2 tablespoons white wine vinegar
2 tablespoons Worcestershire sauce
1 teaspoon dried thyme
3/4 teaspoon ground allspice

3 teaspoons vegetable oil
1/2 teaspoon salt
1 1/4 pounds skinless, boneless
   chicken breast halves, cut into
   12 equal pieces
1 medium red pepper, cut into
   1-inch pieces
4 (12-inch) metal skewers

1. Prepare outdoor grill for direct grilling over medium heat.

2. Coarsely chop 2 green onions; cut remaining 3 green onions into 2-inch-long pieces and reserve. In blender at high speed or in mini food processor, with sharp side of blade facing up, process chopped green onions, jalapeño, ginger, vinegar, Worcestershire, thyme, allspice, 2 teaspoons oil, and 1/4 teaspoon salt until blended, scraping down side of blender once. Transfer herb mixture to medium bowl; add chicken pieces and toss until evenly coated.

3. In small bowl, toss red pepper and green-onion pieces with remaining 1 teaspoon oil and remaining 1/4 teaspoon salt.

4. Alternately thread chicken, red pepper, and green onions onto metal skewers.

5. Place kabobs on hot grill rack over medium heat; brush with any remaining marinade. Grill kabobs, turning to sear on all sides, until juices run clear when chicken is pierced with tip of knife, 10 to 12 minutes.

Each serving: About 200 calories, 27g protein, 6g carbohydrate, 7g total fat (1g saturated), 72mg cholesterol, 440mg sodium.

Jerk Chicken Kabobs

Herbed Chicken
Breasts with Mustard Sauce

Herbed Chicken Breasts with Mustard Sauce

Serve these tasty cutlets with a creamy, slightly sweet mustard sauce and pumpernickel bread for a meal inspired by Swedish gravlax, which is traditionally prepared with salmon.

PREP: 25 MINUTES   GRILL: 8 TO 10 MINUTES   MAKES 4 SERVINGS

MUSTARD SAUCE
2 tablespoons light mayonnaise
1 tablespoon chopped fresh dill
1 tablespoon chopped fresh mint
1 tablespoon Dijon mustard
1 tablespoon white wine vinegar
1 teaspoon sugar

CHICKEN BREASTS
4 medium skinless, boneless chicken
  breast halves (about 1 1/4 pounds)

2 tablespoons sugar
2 tablespoons chopped fresh dill
1 tablespoon chopped fresh mint
2 tablespoons white wine vinegar
1 teaspoon salt
1 teaspoon vegetable oil
1/4 teaspoon coarsely ground
  black pepper

4 slices pumpernickel bread, warmed

1. Prepare outdoor grill for direct grilling over medium-high heat.
2. Prepare mustard sauce: In small bowl, mix mayonnaise, dill, mint, mustard, vinegar, and sugar until blended; set aside.
3. Prepare chicken: If necessary, pound breasts to uniform 1/4-inch thickness. In medium bowl, stir sugar, dill, mint, vinegar, salt, oil, and pepper until mixed. Add chicken; toss until evenly coated.
4. Place chicken on hot grill rack over medium-high heat and grill, turning over once, until juices run clear when thickest part of breast is pierced with tip of knife, 8 to 10 minutes.
5. Serve chicken with mustard sauce and pumpernickel bread.

Each serving: About 330 calories, 36g protein, 23g carbohydrate, 9g total fat (2g saturated), 93mg cholesterol, 955mg sodium.

Chicken and Beef Saté

For a festive outdoor buffet, prepare several different salads and a large bowl of rice to serve alongside the saté. This tasty chicken and beef saté may also be served as an appetizer.

PREP: 45 MINUTES PLUS MARINATING   GRILL: 3 TO 7 MINUTES PER BATCH
MAKES 6 SERVINGS

1 pound skinless, boneless chicken breast halves
1 boneless beef top sirloin steak, 1 inch thick (about 1 1/4 pounds)
2 large limes
1/4 cup plus 1 tablespoon soy sauce
1 tablespoon grated, peeled fresh ginger
2 teaspoons sugar

2 garlic cloves, crushed with garlic press
1/4 cup creamy peanut butter
1/4 cup very hot tap water
4 teaspoons seasoned rice vinegar
1 tablespoon light (mild) molasses
1/8 teaspoon crushed red pepper
Cucumber Relish (page 235)
24 (12-inch) metal skewers

1. Cut chicken breasts lengthwise into 3/4-inch-wide strips; place in a bowl. Holding knife almost parallel to work surface, slice steak crosswise into thin strips; place in separate bowl.

2. From limes, grate 2 teaspoons peel and squeeze 2 tablespoons juice. In small bowl, with fork, mix lime peel, lime juice, 1/4 cup soy sauce, ginger, sugar, and garlic. Stir half of soy-sauce mixture into chicken. Stir remaining soy-sauce mixture into beef. Cover both bowls and let stand 30 minutes in the refrigerator.

3. Prepare outdoor grill for direct grilling over medium heat.

4. Meanwhile, in medium bowl, with wire whisk or fork, mix peanut butter, hot water, rice vinegar, remaining 1 tablespoon soy sauce, molasses, and crushed red pepper until smooth.

5. Prepare Cucumber Relish.

6. Separately thread chicken strips and beef strips, accordion-style, onto metal skewers.

7. Place skewers on hot grill rack over medium heat and grill, turning once, until just cooked through, 3 to 7 minutes. Serve with peanut sauce and Cucumber Relish.

Each serving: About 370 calories, 39g protein, 11g carbohydrate, 19g total fat (5g saturated), 101mg cholesterol, 920mg sodium.

TIP: For variety, try strips of boneless pork loin instead of beef. Cook pork satés, turning once, until cooked through, about 8 minutes.

Chicken and Beef Saté

Thai Chicken Saté

Chicken marinated in curried coconut-milk is teamed with pickled cucumbers and creamy peanut sauce.

PREP: 45 MINUTES   GRILL: 5 TO 8 MINUTES   MAKES 4 SERVINGS

1 English (seedless) cucumber, thinly sliced crosswise
1 1/2 teaspoons salt
1 tablespoon Thai green curry paste
1/4 cup plus 1/3 cup well-stirred unsweetened coconut milk (not cream of coconut)
4 medium skinless, boneless chicken breast halves (about 1 1/4 pounds), each cut diagonally into 6 strips
1/4 cup creamy peanut butter

2 teaspoons soy sauce
1 teaspoon packed dark brown sugar
1/8 teaspoon ground red pepper (cayenne)
1 tablespoon hot water
1/4 cup rice vinegar
3 tablespoons granulated sugar
2 medium shallots, thinly sliced
1 jalapeño chile, seeded and membrane discarded, minced
12 (12-inch) metal skewers

1. In medium bowl, toss cucumber with salt; let stand 30 minutes at room temperature.

2. In another bowl, stir the curry paste and 1/4 cup coconut milk until blended. Add chicken and turn to coat. Let stand 15 minutes at room temperature; stirring occasionally.

3. Prepare outdoor grill for covered direct grilling over medium heat.

4. Meanwhile, prepare peanut sauce: In small bowl, with wire whisk, mix peanut butter, soy sauce, brown sugar, ground red pepper, remaining 1/3 cup coconut milk, and hot water until blended and smooth. Transfer sauce to serving bowl. Makes about 2/3 cup.

5. Drain cucumber, discarding liquid in bowl. Pat cucumber dry with paper towels. Return cucumber to bowl; stir in vinegar, granulated sugar, shallots, and jalapeño; cover and refrigerate until ready to serve.

6. Thread 2 chicken strips, accordion-style, on each of 12 metal skewers; discard marinade. Place skewers on hot grill rack over medium heat. Cover grill and cook, turning skewers once, just until chicken loses its pink color throughout, 5 to 8 minutes.

7. Arrange skewers on platter. Serve with peanut sauce and cucumbers.

Each serving without peanut sauce: About 260 calories, 34g protein, 15g carbohydrate, 6g total fat (3g saturated), 90mg cholesterol, 525mg sodium.

Each tablespoon peanut sauce: About 50 calories, 2g protein, 2g carbohydrate, 5g total fat (2g saturated), 0mg cholesterol, 90mg sodium.

Grilled Chicken Breasts with Tomato-Olive Relish

Our tasty no-cook relish was inspired by Italian puttanesca sauce. Serve with a crisp green vegetable or a side dish of Mediterranean Grilled Eggplant and Summer Squash (page 194).

PREP: 15 MINUTES   GRILL: 10 TO 12 MINUTES   MAKES 4 SERVINGS

2 ripe medium tomatoes, chopped into 1/4-inch pieces
1/4 cup Kalamata olives, pitted and coarsely chopped
2 tablespoons minced red onion
2 tablespoons capers, drained
1 teaspoon red wine vinegar
3 teaspoons olive oil
4 small skinless, boneless chicken breast halves (about 1 pound)
1/4 teaspoon salt
1/4 teaspoon coarsely ground black pepper
Kalamata olives for garnish

1. In small bowl, mix tomatoes, olives, red onion, capers, vinegar, and 1 teaspoon olive oil; set aside.
2. Prepare outdoor grill for direct grilling over medium heat.
3. In medium bowl, toss chicken breasts with salt, pepper, and remaining 2 teaspoons oil until evenly coated.
4. Place chicken on hot grill rack over medium heat and grill, turning once, until juices run clear when thickest part of chicken is pierced with tip of knife, 5 to 6 minutes per side.
5. To serve, top chicken with tomato-olive relish and garnish with olives.

Each serving: About 200 calories, 27g protein, 5g carbohydrate, 7g total fat (1g saturated), 66mg cholesterol, 565mg sodium.

TIP: If you'd like, double the tomato-olive mixture and toss half with 8 ounces cooked corkscrew pasta. Serve the pasta at room temperature alongside the chicken.

Peking Chicken Roll-Ups

The traditional Chinese recipe for duck is labor-intensive and takes several days to make. Our version, prepared in minutes, is made with grilled boneless chicken thighs and served in flour tortillas with hoisin sauce.

PREP: 25 MINUTES   GRILL: 10 TO 12 MINUTES   MAKES 4 SERVINGS

8 (8-inch) flour tortillas
2 tablespoons honey
2 tablespoons soy sauce
1 tablespoon grated, peeled fresh
  ginger
1/8 teaspoon ground red pepper
  (cayenne)
2 garlic cloves, crushed with
  garlic press

6 skinless, boneless chicken thighs
  (about 1 1/4 pounds)
1 teaspoon vegetable oil
1/4 cup hoisin sauce
1/2 English (seedless) cucumber,
  cut into 2" by 1/4" sticks
2 green onions, thinly sliced

1. Prepare outdoor grill for direct grilling over medium-high heat.
2. Stack tortillas and wrap in foil. In small bowl, mix honey, soy sauce, ginger, ground red pepper, and garlic until blended. Set aside tortillas and honey mixture.
3. Coat chicken with oil and place on hot grill rack over medium-high heat. Grill, turning once, 5 minutes. Brush chicken all over with honey mixture, and grill, turning once, or until juices run clear when thickest part of thigh is pierced with tip of knife, 5 to 7 minutes longer.
4. While chicken is cooking, place foil-wrapped tortillas on same grill rack and heat until warm, 3 to 5 minutes.
5. Transfer chicken to cutting board and thinly slice. Spread hoisin sauce on one side of tortillas. Top with chicken, cucumber, and green onions; roll up to serve.

Each serving: About 400 calories, 27g protein, 50g carbohydrate, 10g total fat (3g saturated), 75mg cholesterol, 1,255mg sodium.

Peking Chicken Roll-Ups

Port and Black Currant– Glazed Chicken Thighs

A robust combination of Port, Dijon mustard, and fresh tarragon makes a delectable quick marinade for these chicken thighs. A last-minute brush with a black currant–jelly glaze adds a glisten.

PREP: 15 MINUTES PLUS MARINATING   GRILL: 25 TO 27 MINUTES
MAKES 4 SERVINGS

1/3 cup ruby Port
1/4 cup Dijon mustard
1/2 teaspoon salt
1/4 teaspoon coarsely ground
   black pepper
2 tablespoons chopped fresh
   tarragon

8 medium bone-in chicken thighs
   (about 2 1/2 pounds), skin
   removed
1/4 cup black currant jelly

1. Prepare outdoor grill for direct grilling over medium heat.

2. In large bowl, with wire whisk, mix Port, mustard, salt, pepper, and 1 tablespoon tarragon until blended. Transfer 3 tablespoons marinade to small bowl.

3. Add chicken to marinade in large bowl; toss until evenly coated. Cover bowl and let stand 15 minutes at room temperature or 30 minutes in the refrigerator.

4. Meanwhile, whisk black currant jelly into marinade in small bowl until blended; set aside.

5. Place chicken on hot grill rack over medium heat, and grill, turning once, until juices run clear when thickest part of thigh is pierced with tip of knife, 25 minutes. Brush jelly mixture all over chicken; grill, turning once, until glazed, 1 to 2 minutes longer. Transfer chicken to platter; sprinkle with remaining 1 tablespoon tarragon.

Each serving: About 280 calories, 28g protein, 15g carbohydrate, 12g total fat (3g saturated), 99mg cholesterol, 290mg sodium.

Five-Spice Chicken Thighs with Plum Chutney

Usually served with curry, chutney is also an excellent accompaniment for this Asian-spiced chicken.

PREP: 20 MINUTES PLUS CHILLING   GRILL: 18 MINUTES
MAKES 4 SERVINGS

PLUM CHUTNEY
1 pound ripe plums (about 4 medium), pitted and cut into 1/4-inch pieces

1/4 cup lightly packed fresh basil leaves, chopped

2 tablespoons balsamic vinegar

1 tablespoon minced red onion

2 teaspoons sugar

1 teaspoon grated, peeled fresh ginger

1/8 teaspoon salt

CHICKEN THIGHS
8 small bone-in chicken thighs (about 2 pounds), skin removed

1 teaspoon salt

1 garlic clove, crushed with garlic press

2 1/2 teaspoons Chinese five-spice powder

3 tablespoons orange marmalade

1 tablespoon water

1. Prepare chutney: In medium bowl, stir plums, basil, vinegar, onion, sugar, ginger, and salt until well mixed. Cover and refrigerate at least 1 hour or up to 1 day. Makes about 2 1/2 cups.

2. Meanwhile, prepare outdoor grill for covered direct grilling over medium heat.

3. Prepare chicken thighs: In medium bowl, toss chicken with salt, garlic, and 2 teaspoons five-spice powder. In cup, mix marmalade with remaining 1/2 teaspoon five-spice powder and water.

4. Spray chicken with nonstick cooking spray. Place chicken on hot grill rack over medium heat. Cover grill and cook chicken, turning once, 16 minutes. Brush chicken with half of marmalade mixture; turn chicken and cook, uncovered, 1 minute. Brush chicken with remaining marmalade mixture; turn and cook until juices run clear when thickest part of thigh is pierced with tip of knife, about 1 minute longer. Serve with plum chutney.

Each serving chicken: About 290 calories, 27g protein, 11g carbohydrate, 11g total fat (4g saturated), 99mg cholesterol, 685mg sodium.

Each 1/4 cup chutney: About 30 calories, 0g protein, 7g carbohydrate, 0g total fat (1g saturated), 0mg cholesterol, 30mg sodium.

Summer Squash and Chicken

For this easy summer supper, simply toss the sliced squash on the grill along with the marinated chicken. You can use zucchini, yellow squash, or a combination.

PREP: 15 MINUTES PLUS MARINATING   GRILL: 10 MINUTES
MAKES 4 SERVINGS

1 lemon
1 tablespoon olive oil
1/2 teaspoon salt
1/4 teaspoon coarsely ground
   black pepper
4 medium skinless, boneless chicken
   thighs (about 1 1/4 pounds)

4 medium yellow summer squash
   and/or zucchini (about 6 ounces
   each), each cut lengthwise into
   4 wedges
1/4 cup snipped fresh chives

1. From lemon, grate 1 tablespoon peel and squeeze 3 tablespoons juice. In medium bowl, whisk together lemon peel and juice, oil, salt, and pepper; transfer 2 tablespoons marinade to cup.

2. Add chicken thighs to bowl with lemon-juice marinade; toss until evenly coated. Cover and let stand 15 minutes at room temperature or 30 minutes in the refrigerator.

3. Meanwhile, prepare outdoor grill for covered direct grilling over medium heat.

4. Discard chicken marinade. Place chicken and squash on hot grill rack. Cover grill and cook over medium heat, turning chicken and squash over once and removing pieces as they are done, until juices run clear when thickest part of thigh is pierced with tip of knife and squash is tender and browned, 10 to 12 minutes.

5. Transfer chicken and squash to cutting board. Cut chicken into 1-inch-wide strips; cut each squash wedge crosswise in half.

6. To serve, on large platter, toss squash with reserved lemon-juice marinade, then toss with chicken and sprinkle with chives.

Each serving: About 255 calories, 29g protein, 8g carbohydrate, 8g total fat (3g saturated), 101mg cholesterol, 240mg sodium.

Summer Squash and Chicken

Portuguese Mixed Grill

We've used chorizo instead of the less readily available Portuguese sausage—linguiça. Chorizo, a spicy Spanish sausage, is often available in packages of two in the meat or deli section of your supermarket. Be sure to purchase fully cooked chorizo.

PREP: 30 MINUTES PLUS MARINATING   GRILL: 25 MINUTES
MAKES 6 SERVINGS

1/4 cup red wine vinegar
1 teaspoon salt
1/2 teaspoon coarsely ground
   black pepper
3 tablespoons olive oil
2 tablespoons chopped fresh oregano
8 large bone-in chicken thighs (about
   3 pounds), skin removed

3 medium red onions
3 (12-inch) metal skewers
3/4 pound fully cooked chorizo
   sausage links, each cut
   crosswise in half
2/3 cup assorted olives such as
   Kalamata, cracked green, and
   Picholine (optional)

1. In large bowl, combine vinegar, salt, pepper, 2 tablespoons oil, and 1 tablespoon chopped oregano. Add chicken thighs; toss until evenly coated. Cover and let stand 30 minutes in the refrigerator.

2. Prepare outdoor grill for direct grilling over medium heat.

3. Meanwhile, cut each red onion into 6 wedges; thread onto 3 metal skewers.

4. Place red-onion skewers on hot grill rack over medium heat. Brush with remaining 1 tablespoon oil; grill 5 minutes. Place chicken thighs on grill with onions; grill, turning onions and chicken once, until onions are browned and tender and juices run clear when chicken thighs are pierced with tip of knife, about 20 minutes longer.

5. About 10 minutes before onions and chicken are done, add chorizo pieces to grill and cook, turning chorizo occasionally, until lightly browned and heated through.

6. To serve, place red-onion skewers on platter with chicken and chorizo. Sprinkle with remaining 1 tablespoon chopped oregano and serve with olives, if you like.

Each serving: About 550 calories, 48g protein, 10g carbohydrate, 35g total fat (11g saturated), 187mg cholesterol, 1,240mg sodium.

Portuguese Mixed Grill

Grilled Thai Chicken Salad

Add zest to boneless chicken with a spicy Thai blend, then grill it and slice for a delicious main-course salad

PREP: 30 MINUTES   GRILL: 10 TO 12 MINUTES   MAKES 4 SERVINGS

THAI DRESSING

2 tablespoons fresh lime juice

4 teaspoons Asian fish sauce (nuoc nam)

1 tablespoon reduced-sodium soy sauce

1 teaspoon sugar

CHICKEN SALAD

4 large skinless, boneless chicken thighs (about 1 1/2 pounds)

2 tablespoons Thai seasoning

2 bags (10 ounces each) torn romaine lettuce leaves

2 cups loosely packed fresh mint leaves

2 papayas or mangoes or 1 of each, peeled, seeded, and sliced

2 green onions, sliced

1. Prepare outdoor grill for direct grilling over medium heat.

2. Prepare dressing: In cup, combine lime juice, fish sauce, soy sauce, and sugar; set aside.

3. Prepare chicken salad: In medium bowl, toss chicken with Thai seasoning. Place chicken on hot grill rack over medium heat; grill, turning once, until juices run clear when thickest part of thigh is pierced with tip of knife, 10 to 12 minutes.

4. In large bowl, toss lettuce, mint, papaya, and green onions with dressing. Thinly slice chicken. Divide salad among 4 dinner plates. Top with chicken slices.

Each serving: About 375 calories, 38g protein, 24g carbohydrate, 15g total fat (4g saturated), 121mg cholesterol, 1,215mg sodium.

TIP: Seasoning mixes vary among manufacturers, especially with regard to sodium content. Add salt to taste if necessary.

Chicken Caesar Salad

This classic restaurant-style salad is enhanced with the smoky flavor of grilled chicken and homemade crusty croutons.

PREP: 25 MINUTES   GRILL: 15 MINUTES   MAKES 4 SERVINGS

1 lemon
1 small garlic clove, crushed with
  garlic press
1 teaspoon Worcestershire sauce
1 teaspoon Dijon mustard
1/2 teaspoon anchovy paste
3 tablespoons plus 1 teaspoon
  olive oil
1 teaspoon salt
1/2 teaspoon coarsely ground
  black pepper

4 medium skinless, boneless chicken
  breast halves (about 1 1/4 pounds)
1/2 loaf French bread (4 ounces),
  cut lengthwise in half
1 large head romaine lettuce (about
  1 1/4 pounds), torn into bite-size
  pieces
1/4 cup freshly grated Parmesan
  cheese

1. Prepare outdoor grill for direct grilling over medium heat.
2. From lemon, grate 2 teaspoons peel and squeeze 2 tablespoons juice.
3. In small bowl, with wire whisk, mix garlic, Worcestershire, mustard, anchovy paste, lemon juice, 3 tablespoons oil, 1/2 teaspoon salt, and 1/4 teaspoon pepper; set aside dressing.
4. Rub chicken with lemon peel and remaining 1 teaspoon oil; sprinkle with remaining 1/2 teaspoon salt and 1/4 teaspoon pepper. Gently place chicken and bread, cut side down, on hot grill rack over medium heat. Toast bread, turning once, until golden, about 5 minutes. Grill chicken, turning once, until juices run clear when thickest part of breast is pierced with tip of knife, 12 to 15 minutes. Transfer bread and chicken to cutting board. Cut chicken into 1/2-inch-thick slices. Cut bread into 1-inch cubes to make croutons.
5. To serve, in large bowl, toss chicken with 1 tablespoon dressing. Add lettuce, Parmesan, croutons, and remaining dressing; toss until well coated.

Each serving: About 405 calories, 40g protein, 20g carbohydrate, 18g total fat (4g saturated), 95mg cholesterol, 995mg sodium.

Grilled Chicken and Mango Salad

If mangoes are not available, try firm, ripe nectarines, plums, peaches, or a combination of all three.

PREP: 30 MINUTES PLUS MARINATING   GRILL: 12 TO 15 MINUTES
MAKES 4 SERVINGS

1/4 cup olive oil

1/4 cup seasoned rice vinegar

3/4 teaspoon salt

1/4 teaspoon ground red pepper (cayenne)

4 medium bone-in chicken thighs (1 1/2 pounds)

1 large shallot, minced

1/4 cup loosely packed fresh cilantro leaves, chopped

1 tablespoon chopped fresh mint

1 tablespoon minced, peeled fresh ginger

1/2 teaspoon freshly grated lemon peel

1 mango, peeled, pitted, and cut into 1/4-inch pieces

1 Kirby cucumber (about 5 ounces), cut into 1/4-inch pieces

4 medium ears corn, husks and silk removed

10 cups mixed baby greens (5 ounces)

1. In medium bowl, with wire whisk or fork, mix oil, vinegar, salt, and ground red pepper. Spoon 3 tablespoons oil mixture into pie plate. Add chicken to mixture in pie plate; turn to coat. Let stand, turning once, 15 minutes at room temperature or 30 minutes in the refrigerator.

2. Prepare outdoor grill for direct grilling over medium heat.

3. Meanwhile, stir shallot, cilantro, mint, ginger, and lemon peel into oil mixture in bowl. Stir in mango and cucumber; set aside.

4. Place chicken on hot grill rack over medium heat; discard marinade in pie plate. Grill chicken, turning once, until juices run clear when thickest part is pierced with tip of knife, 12 to 15 minutes. At the same time, grill corn, turning often, until lightly browned, 10 to 15 minutes. Transfer chicken and corn to plate; set aside until cool enough to handle.

5. When cool, remove and discard skin and bones from chicken thighs. With fingers, pull meat into shreds. With sharp knife, cut kernels from corncobs. Toss chicken and corn with mango mixture.

6. To serve, divide greens among 4 plates; top with chicken mixture.

Each serving: About 385 calories, 23g protein, 37g carbohydrate, 18g total fat (4g saturated), 70mg cholesterol, 655mg sodium.

Grilled Chicken Taco Salad

A great way to prepare this Mexican favorite during the summer: Spicy chicken breasts are first grilled and then served over black-bean salsa, shredded lettuce, and crisp corn tortillas.

PREP: 25 MINUTES   GRILL: 8 TO 10 MINUTES   MAKES 4 SERVINGS

1 can (15 to 19 ounces) black beans, rinsed and drained
3/4 cup medium-hot salsa
1 tablespoon fresh lime juice
1 cup loosely packed fresh cilantro leaves, chopped
2 tablespoons chili powder
1 teaspoon ground cumin
1 teaspoon ground coriander
1 teaspoon brown sugar
1/2 teaspoon salt
1/4 teaspoon ground red pepper (cayenne)
1 tablespoon olive oil
1 pound skinless, boneless chicken breast halves
4 corn tortillas
4 cups thinly sliced lettuce
lime wedges, avocado slices, and sour cream (optional)

1. Prepare outdoor grill for direct grilling over medium-high heat.
2. In medium bowl, mix beans, salsa, lime juice, and half of cilantro; set aside.
3. In cup, stir chili powder, cumin, coriander, sugar, salt, ground red pepper, and oil until evenly mixed (mixture will be dry).
4. If necessary, pound breast halves to uniform 1/4-inch thickness. With hands, rub chicken with chili-powder mixture.
5. Place chicken on hot grill rack over medium-high heat and grill, turning once, until juices run clear when thickest part of breast is pierced with tip of knife, 8 to 10 minutes. Place corn tortillas on grill rack with chicken and cook, turning once, until lightly browned, 3 to 5 minutes. Transfer chicken to cutting board. Place tortillas on 4 dinner plates.
6. Cut chicken into long thin strips. Top tortillas with lettuce, bean mixture, and chicken strips. Sprinkle with remaining cilantro. If you like, serve with lime wedges, avocado slices, and sour cream.

Each serving: About 370 calories, 35g protein, 45g carbohydrate, 8g total fat (2g saturated), 72mg cholesterol, 1,075mg sodium.

Grilled Chicken and Pepper Salad

A great summer salad combo—grilled chicken breasts, red peppers, and onions all tossed in a tangy balsamic vinaigrette with arugula leaves.

PREP: 15 MINUTES   GRILL: 20 MINUTES   MAKES 4 SERVINGS

BALSAMIC VINAIGRETTE
- 3 tablespoons olive oil
- 2 tablespoons balsamic vinegar
- 1 small garlic clove, crushed with garlic press
- 1 teaspoon Dijon mustard
- 1/2 teaspoon sugar
- 1/2 teaspoon salt
- 1/4 teaspoon coarsely ground black pepper

VEGETABLES AND CHICKEN
- 2 red peppers
- 2 yellow peppers
- 1 large red onion (12 ounces), cut into 8 wedges
- 4 teaspoons olive oil
- 1 pound skinless, boneless chicken breast halves
- 1/4 teaspoon salt
- 1/4 teaspoon coarsely ground black pepper
- 1 cup grape tomatoes
- 1 bunch arugula (about 4 ounces), tough stems removed

1. Prepare outdoor grill for direct grilling over medium heat.

2. Prepare vinaigrette: In serving bowl, with wire whisk, blend oil, vinegar, garlic, mustard, sugar, salt, and pepper; set aside.

3. Prepare vegetables and chicken: Cut each pepper lengthwise in half; discard stems and seeds. With hand, flatten each pepper half. In bowl, toss peppers and onion wedges with 3 teaspoons oil. Rub chicken breasts with remaining 1 teaspoon oil; sprinkle with salt and pepper.

4. Place chicken on hot grill rack over medium heat and grill, turning once, until juices run clear when thickest part of breast is pierced with tip of knife, 12 to 15 minutes.

5. While chicken is cooking, place onion wedges and peppers, skin side down, on same grill rack. Cook onion, turning occasionally, until golden, about 15 minutes; cook peppers until skins are charred and blistered, 18 to 20 minutes.

6. When onion wedges are done, transfer to plate. When chicken is done, transfer to cutting board. When peppers are done, wrap in foil and allow

them to steam at room temperature until cool enough to handle, about 10 minutes.

7. While peppers are steaming, cut chicken breasts crosswise into 1/2-inch-wide strips.

8. Remove peppers from foil; discard skins. Cut peppers lengthwise into thin slices. Add peppers, chicken, onion, tomatoes, and arugula to bowl with dressing; toss gently to coat.

Each serving: About 330 calories, 29g protein, 18 carbohydrate, 16g total fat (3g saturated), 72mg cholesterol, 520mg sodium.

Grilled Chicken and Pepper Salad

Chicken Burgers

If you're looking for plain, straightforward burgers, we've got them. We also have suggestions to jazz them up to please a variety of cravings, so pick your favorite flavor family: teriyaki, barbecue, or herb.

PREP: 20 MINUTES   GRILL: 12 MINUTES   MAKES 4 SERVINGS

BASIC BURGERS
1 pound ground chicken breasts
1 medium carrot, peeled and grated
  (1/2 cup)
2 green onions, minced

1 garlic clove, crushed with
  garlic press
4 hamburger buns, warmed
sliced cucumber, lettuce leaves, and
  green onion (optional)

1. Prepare outdoor grill for direct grilling over medium heat.
2. Prepare burgers: In medium bowl, combine ground chicken, carrot, minced green onions, and garlic.
3. On waxed paper, shape chicken mixture into four 3 1/2-inch round patties (mixture will be very soft and moist).
4. Place patties on hot grill rack over medium heat and grill, turning once, until juices run clear when center of burger is pierced with tip of knife, about 12 minutes. (If you have a grill with widely spaced grates, you may want to place burgers on a perforated grill topper to keep them intact.)
5. Place burgers on warmed buns. Serve with cucumber slices, lettuce leaves, and green onions, if you like.

Each serving: About 275 calories, 30g protein, 24g carbohydrate, 5g total fat (1g saturated), 72mg cholesterol, 310mg sodium.

Teriyaki Burgers

Prepare Basic Burgers as directed, but add *2 tablespoons soy sauce; 1 tablespoon seasoned rice vinegar; 2 teaspoons grated, peeled fresh ginger; and 2 teaspoons Asian sesame oil* to ground chicken mixture in Step 2. (Prepare burger mixture just before cooking to prevent ginger from changing texture of meat.)

Each serving: About 305 calories, 31g protein, 26g carbohydrate, 8g total fat (2g saturated), 72mg cholesterol, 940mg sodium.

Chicken Burgers

Barbecue Burgers

Prepare Basic Burgers as directed, but add *2 tablespoons chili sauce*; *1 tablespoon light (mild) molasses*; *2 teaspoons cayenne pepper sauce*; *2 teaspoons Worcestershire sauce*; and *1/4 teaspoon salt* to ground chicken mixture in Step 2.

Each serving: About 295 calories, 31g protein, 30g carbohydrate, 5g total fat (1g saturated), 72mg cholesterol, 715mg sodium.

Herb Burgers

Prepare Basic Burgers as directed, but add *2 tablespoons finely chopped fresh dill*; *1 tablespoon dried mint*; *1 tablespoon fresh lemon juice*; *1 teaspoon ground cumin*; *1/2 teaspoon salt*; and *1/8 teaspoon ground red pepper (cayenne)* to ground chicken mixture in Step 2.

Each serving: About 280 calories, 31g protein, 25g carbohydrate, 5g total fat (1g saturated), 72mg cholesterol, 605mg sodium.

Mediterranean Chicken Sandwiches

The flavors of the Mediterranean give this sandwich its special zip. Use the olive mayonnaise as a spread for beef or chicken sandwiches as well. Double the grilled flavor and grill the bread too. Cut bread as directed, then grill pieces for about 1 1/2 minutes per side before spreading them with the mayonnaise mixture.

PREP: 25 MINUTES   GRILL: 10 TO 12 MINUTES   MAKES 4 SERVINGS

1 teaspoon fennel seeds
1/2 teaspoon dried thyme
1/2 teaspoon salt
1/4 teaspoon coarsely ground
  black pepper
4 medium skinless, boneless chicken
  breast halves (about 1 1/4 pounds)

1/4 cup Kalamata olives, pitted
  and minced
2 tablespoons mayonnaise
1 loaf (8 ounces) Italian bread
2 small tomatoes, each cut into
  4 slices

1. Prepare outdoor grill for direct grilling over medium heat.
2. In mortar with pestle, crush fennel seeds with thyme, salt, and pepper. Rub both sides of chicken breasts with fennel-seed mixture; set aside.
3. In small bowl, mix olives and mayonnaise. Cut bread crosswise into 4 equal pieces, then cut each piece horizontally in half. Spread olive mixture evenly on cut sides of bread; set aside.
4. Place chicken on hot grill rack over medium heat and grill, turning once, until juices run clear when thickest part is pierced with tip of knife, 10 to 12 minutes. Transfer chicken to cutting board.
5. To assemble sandwiches, cut chicken breasts crosswise into 1/4-inch-thick slices. On bottom halves of bread, layer sliced chicken and tomatoes. Replace top halves of bread.

Each serving: About 400 calories, 38g protein, 32g carbohydrate, 12g total fat (2g saturated), 86mg cholesterol, 910mg sodium.

Cornish Hens with Ginger-Plum Glaze

The hens are cut in half for fast, even cooking, then brushed with a gingery plum jam. Glazed plum halves are grilled right alongside. Tossed in the jam-ginger mixture and grilled by themselves, the glazed plums would be a fine finish to any summer barbecue.

PREP: 25 MINUTES   GRILL: ABOUT 30 MINUTES   MAKES 4 SERVINGS

2/3 cup plum jam or preserves

3 teaspoons grated, peeled fresh ginger

4 large plums, each cut in half and pitted

2 Cornish hens (about 1 3/4 pounds each)

2 tablespoons reduced-sodium soy sauce

1 teaspoon Chinese five-spice powder

3/4 teaspoon salt

1/4 teaspoon coarsely ground black pepper

2 small garlic cloves, crushed with garlic press

1. Prepare outdoor grill for direct grilling over medium heat.

2. In 1-quart saucepan, heat plum jam and 1 teaspoon ginger over low heat, stirring, until jam has melted, 1 to 2 minutes. Spoon 2 tablespoons plum glaze into medium bowl; add plums and toss to coat. Set glaze aside.

3. Remove giblets and necks from hens; refrigerate for another use. With kitchen shears, cut each hen in half. Rinse with cold running water and drain well; pat dry with paper towels.

4. In small bowl, mix remaining 2 teaspoons ginger with soy sauce, five-spice powder, salt, pepper, and garlic. Brush mixture on hen halves.

5. Place hen halves, skin side down, on hot grill rack over medium heat and grill, turning once, 15 minutes. Brush skin side of hens with plum glaze from saucepan; turn hens over and grill 5 minutes. Brush hens with remaining glaze; turn and grill until juices run clear when thickest part of thigh is pierced with tip of knife and hens are golden, about 10 minutes longer.

6. Just before hens are done, place plums on same grill rack and cook, turning once, until plums are hot and lightly browned, about 6 minutes.

7. Serve each hen half with 2 plum halves.

Each serving: About 620 calories, 39g protein, 47g carbohydrate, 31g total fat (8g saturated), 219mg cholesterol, 920mg sodium.

Turkey on the Grill

This easy method yields tender meat, crispy skin, and smoky flavor. When turkey is cooked on a covered grill, there may be a rosy-pink band of meat just under the skin. This doesn't mean the meat is undercooked—it's a result of charcoal combustion reacting with the pigment in the meat.

PREP: 15 MINUTES   GRILL: 2 HOURS 15 MINUTES TO 3 HOURS
MAKES 12 SERVINGS

1 fresh or frozen (thawed) turkey (12 pounds), giblets and neck removed
2 tablespoons vegetable oil
2 teaspoons dried sage
2 teaspoons dried thyme
2 teaspoons salt
1/2 teaspoon coarsely ground black pepper

1. Prepare grill: In bottom of covered charcoal grill, with vents open and grill uncovered, ignite 60 charcoal briquettes (not self-starting). Allow briquettes to burn until all coals are covered with a thin coat of gray ash in the center of grill about 30 minutes. Push briquettes to two opposite sides of grill and arrange into two piles. Place sturdy disposable foil pan (about 13" by 9" by 2") between piles of coals to catch drips.
2. Rinse turkey inside and out with cold running water and drain well; pat dry with paper towels. Fasten neck skin to back with one or two skewers. With breast side up, fold wings under back of turkey. Tie legs and tail together with string, push drumsticks under band of skin, or use stuffing clamp. In cup, mix oil, sage, thyme, salt, and pepper; rub spice mixture on outside of turkey.
3. Place turkey, breast side up, on hot grill rack directly over foil pan. Cover grill and roast turkey 2 hours 15 minutes to 3 hours, adding 8 or 9 briquettes to each side of grill every hour to maintain a grill temperature of 325°F on oven or grill thermometer. Roast until meat thermometer registers 180° to 185°F and juices run clear when thickest part of thigh is pierced with tip of knife.
4. Transfer turkey to warm platter; let stand 15 minutes to set juices for easier carving. Carefully remove drip pan from grill. If you like, skim and discard fat from drippings; serve drippings along with turkey.

Each serving: About 535 calories, 73g protein, 0g carbohydrate, 25g total fat (7g saturated), 212mg cholesterol, 380mg sodium.

Turkey Cutlets, Indian Style

Delicious with a squeeze of fresh lime or with Mango Salsa (page 224) or Pineapple Salsa (page 223) served alongside. For a festive presentation, set out bowls of yogurt, store-bought mango chutney, fluffy basmati rice, and chopped fresh cilantro alongside the cutlets.

PREP: 15 MINUTES   GRILL: 5 TO 7 MINUTES   MAKES 6 SERVINGS

2 large limes
1/3 cup plain low-fat yogurt
1 tablespoon vegetable oil
2 teaspoons minced, peeled
    fresh ginger
1 teaspoon ground cumin

1 teaspoon ground coriander
1 teaspoon salt
1 garlic clove, crushed with
    garlic press
1 1/2 pounds turkey cutlets

1. Prepare outdoor grill for direct grilling over medium heat.

2. From 1 lime, grate 1 teaspoon peel and squeeze 1 tablespoon juice. Cut remaining lime into wedges; reserve.

3. In large bowl, mix lime peel, lime juice, yogurt, oil, ginger, cumin, coriander, salt, and garlic until blended.

4. Just before grilling, add turkey cutlets to bowl with yogurt mixture; stir to coat. (Do not let cutlets marinate in yogurt mixture; their texture will become mealy.)

5. Place cutlets on hot grill rack over medium heat and grill until they just lose their pink color throughout, 5 to 7 minutes. Serve with lime wedges.

Each serving: About 160 calories, 29g protein, 3g carbohydrate, 3g total fat (1g saturated), 71mg cholesterol, 450mg sodium.

TIP: Freeze any extra unpeeled fresh ginger, wrapped well in plastic wrap. It will keep for up to six months.

Spiced Grilled Turkey Breast

Soaking a whole turkey breast overnight in a spiced salt solution, or brine, produces exceptionally tender and flavorful meat. You can also brine a whole chicken before roasting. Serve with Peach Salsa (page 225).

PREP: 35 MINUTES PLUS BRINING AND STANDING   GRILL: ABOUT 25 MINUTES
MAKES 12 SERVINGS

SPICED TURKEY
1/4 cup sugar
1/4 cup kosher salt
2 tablespoons cracked black pepper
2 tablespoons ground ginger
1 tablespoon ground cinnamon
1 whole boneless turkey breast
   (about 4 pounds), skin removed
   and breast cut in half

4 garlic cloves, crushed with
   side of chef's knife
Peach Salsa (page 225)

HONEY GLAZE
2 tablespoons honey
2 tablespoons Dijon mustard
1 chipotle chile in adobo, minced
1 teaspoon balsamic vinegar

1. Prepare turkey: In 2-quart saucepan, heat sugar, salt, pepper, ginger, cinnamon, and *1 cup water* to boiling over high heat. Reduce heat to low; simmer 2 minutes. Remove from heat; stir in *3 cups ice water.*
2. Place turkey breast in large ziptight plastic bag; add brine and garlic. Seal bag, pressing out excess air. Place bag in bowl and refrigerate breast, turning occasionally, 24 hours.
3. Prepare outdoor grill for covered direct grilling over medium heat.
4. Meanwhile, prepare glaze: In small bowl, stir honey, mustard, chipotle, and vinegar until blended. Set aside.
5. Remove turkey from bag; discard brine and garlic. With paper towels, pat turkey dry and brush off most of pepper. With long-handled basting brush, oil grill rack. Place turkey on hot rack over medium heat. Cover grill and cook turkey, turning once, 20 minutes. Brush turkey with glaze and cook 5 to 10 minutes longer (depending on thickness of breast), brushing and turning frequently, until temperature on meat thermometer inserted into thickest part of breast reaches 165°F. (Internal temperature will rise 5°F upon standing.) Place turkey on cutting board and let rest 10 minutes to set juices for easier slicing.
6. While turkey rests, prepare Peach Salsa (page 225).
7. Serve turkey hot, or cover and refrigerate to serve cold.

Spiced Grilled Turkey Breast

Each serving turkey: About 170 calories, 34g protein, 4g carbohydrate, 1g total fat (0g saturated), 94mg cholesterol, 555mg sodium.

Southwestern Turkey Fajitas

Broiling the tomatillos adds a subtle smokiness to this luscious salsa. Seasoning mixes vary among manufacturers, especially with regard to salt content. Add salt to taste if necessary.

PREP: 20 MINUTES   GRILL: 15 TO 20 MINUTES   MAKES 6 SERVINGS

TOMATILLO SALSA

1 pound tomatillos, husked
 and rinsed
1 small poblano chile, cut in half,
 stems and seeds discarded
1 small shallot, cut up
3 tablespoons fresh lime juice
3/4 teaspoon salt
3/4 teaspoon sugar
1/3 cup packed fresh cilantro leaves,
 chopped

TURKEY AND ONION FAJITAS

2 whole turkey breast tenderloins
 (about 1 3/4 pounds) or 6 medium
 skinless, boneless chicken breast
 halves (about 1 3/4 pounds)
2 tablespoons fajita seasoning
4 teaspoons olive oil
3 large onions (12 ounces each),
 cut into 1/2-inch-thick slices
12 (6-inch) corn tortillas

1. Prepare salsa: Preheat broiler. Place tomatillos in broiling pan without rack. Place pan in broiler 5 to 6 inches from heat source. Broil tomatillos, turning once, until blackened in spots and blistering, about 10 minutes. When tomatillos are turned, add poblano, skin side up, to pan and broil until charred, about 6 minutes.

2. In blender or food processor with knife blade attached, pulse tomatillos, poblano, shallot, lime juice, salt, and sugar until chopped. Stir in cilantro. Cover and refrigerate salsa up to 3 days if not serving right away. Makes about 2 cups.

3. Prepare outdoor grill for direct grilling over medium heat. Prepare fajitas: In medium bowl, toss turkey or chicken with fajita seasoning and 2 teaspoons oil until evenly coated. Brush onion slices with remaining 2 teaspoons oil.

4. Place turkey or chicken and onions on hot grill rack over medium heat. Grill, turning once, until meat thermometer registers 170°F and juices run clear when thickest part of tenderloin is pierced with tip of knife, 15 to 20 minutes for turkey (10 to 12 minutes for chicken). Grill onions, turning once, until tender and golden, 12 to 15 minutes.

5. While turkey or chicken is grilling, place several tortillas on same grill rack and heat just until lightly browned, transferring them to foil as they brown. Wrap tortillas in foil and keep warm.

6. To assemble fajitas: Transfer turkey or chicken to cutting board and thinly slice. Top tortillas with equal amounts of turkey or chicken and onion. Spoon some salsa on each and fold to eat out of hand. Serve with any remaining onions and salsa.

Each serving without salsa: About 350 calories, 36g protein, 35g carbohydrate, 7g total fat (1g saturated), 88mg cholesterol, 440mg sodium.

Each 1/4 cup salsa: About 30 calories, 1g protein, 6g carbohydrate, 1g total fat (0g saturated), 0mg cholesterol, 220mg sodium.

Southwestern Turkey Fajitas

MEAT

Backyard BLTs

Spice-Rubbed Beef Tenderloin

Fennel seeds, with their licoricelike flavor, are similar to anise seeds, but not quite as sweet. Make a double batch of this rub, store it in a cool, dry place out of the sunlight, and use it the next time you're grilling pork chops, pork tenderloin, or a leg of lamb.

PREP: 10 MINUTES   GRILL: 30 TO 40 MINUTES   MAKES 10 SERVINGS

1 tablespoon fennel seeds	1/2 teaspoon crushed red pepper
2 teaspoons salt	1 beef tenderloin roast (about
1/2 teaspoon ground ginger	2 1/2 pounds)

1. Prepare outdoor grill for covered direct grilling over medium heat.

2. In mortar with pestle or in ziptight plastic bag with rolling pin, crush fennel seeds. In small bowl, combine fennel seeds, salt, ginger, and crushed red pepper. With hands, rub beef tenderloin with spice mixture. If you like, place spice-rubbed beef in ziptight plastic bag and refrigerate several hours or overnight before grilling.

3. Place beef on hot grill rack over medium heat. Cover grill and cook beef, turning occasionally, until meat thermometer inserted in center of meat reaches 135°F, 30 to 40 minutes. Internal temperature of meat will rise to 140°F (medium-rare) upon standing. Or cook until meat reaches desired doneness.

4. Transfer tenderloin to cutting board and let stand 10 minutes to set juices for easier slicing.

Each serving: About 225 calories, 19g protein, 0g carbohydrate, 16g total fat (6g saturated), 66mg cholesterol, 510mg sodium.

TIP: Ask your butcher to cut this roast from a whole tenderloin for you. The center-cut roast should be 2 1/2 pounds after trimming; the ends make deliciously tender kabobs.

Barbecued Beef Brisket

This rich barbecued brisket can be made well ahead and then finished on an outdoor grill. Slow-cook the meat on the stovetop up to two days ahead, then glaze with sauce and grill for twenty minutes to heat through. Leftovers, if there are any, can be heated in a little sauce and spooned over crusty rolls.

PREP: 3 HOURS 25 MINUTES   GRILL: 20 MINUTES   MAKES 12 SERVINGS

1 fresh beef brisket (4 1/2 pounds),
    trimmed
1 medium onion, peeled and cut
    into quarters
1 large carrot, peeled and cut into
    1 1/2-inch pieces

1 bay leaf
1 teaspoon whole black peppercorns
1/4 teaspoon whole allspice
Chunky BBQ Sauce (page 219)

1. In 8-quart Dutch oven, place brisket, onion, carrot, bay leaf, peppercorns, and allspice. Add enough *water to cover* and heat to boiling over high heat. Reduce heat to low; cover and simmer until meat is fork-tender, about 3 hours.

2. Meanwhile, prepare Chunky BBQ Sauce.

3. When brisket is done, transfer to platter. If not serving brisket right away, cover and refrigerate until ready to serve.

4. Prepare outdoor grill for direct grilling over medium heat.

5. Place brisket on hot grill rack over medium heat and grill 10 minutes. Turn brisket over and grill 5 minutes. Spoon 1 cup barbecue sauce on top of brisket and cook until brisket is heated through, about 5 minutes longer. (Do not turn brisket after topping with sauce.) If you like, reheat remaining sauce in small saucepan on grill. Thinly slice brisket across grain and serve with sauce.

Each serving with sauce: About 500 calories, 30g protein, 4g carbohydrate, 40g total fat (15g saturated), 117mg cholesterol, 185mg sodium.

TIP: Allspice is available in two forms, whole berries or ground. It gets its name from the fact that it tastes like a combination of cloves, cinnamon, and nutmeg. Try adding a few whole berries to hot spiced cider.

Red Wine and Rosemary Porterhouse

This robust marinade can season a thick, juicy steak in fifteen minutes. Marinate for up to one hour for more intense flavor. It's also good on lamb, pork, or poultry. Serve with Lemon-Garlic Potato Packet (page 201) and Crumb-Topped Tomatoes (page 202).

PREP: 10 MINUTES PLUS MARINATING GRILL: 15 TO 20 MINUTES
MAKES 4 SERVINGS

1/2 cup dry red wine
1 tablespoon Worcestershire sauce
1 tablespoon tomato paste
1 tablespoon Dijon mustard
1 tablespoon balsamic vinegar
1 tablespoon chopped fresh rosemary

1 large garlic clove, crushed with garlic press
1 beef porterhouse or T-bone steak, 1 1/2 inches thick (about 1 1/2 pounds)
1 lemon, cut into wedges

1. In small bowl, stir red wine, Worcestershire, tomato paste, mustard, vinegar, rosemary, and garlic.

2. Place steak in large ziptight plastic bag. Pour red-wine marinade over steak, turning to coat. Seal bag, pressing out excess air. Let stand 15 minutes at room temperature or refrigerate up to 1 hour, turning once.

3. Prepare outdoor grill for direct grilling over medium heat.

4. Remove steak from bag; discard marinade. Place steak on hot grill rack over medium heat and grill, turning once, 15 to 20 minutes for medium-rare or until desired doneness.

5. Transfer steak to cutting board. Let stand 10 minutes at room temperature to allow juices to set for easier slicing. Thinly slice steak and serve with lemon wedges.

Each serving: About 395 calories, 32g protein, 1g carbohydrate, 28g total fat (11g saturated), 104mg cholesterol, 125mg sodium.

TIP: For a dry red wine that would work well in this recipe, try a Shiraz, Merlot, Chianti, or Cabernet.

Pepper-Crusted Filet Mignon

These very tender steaks make great company fare, plus they're a snap to make ahead. Simply coat them with crushed spices as directed, then cover and refrigerate for up to one day until ready to cook.

PREP: 15 MINUTES PLUS STANDING   GRILL: 16 TO 20 MINUTES
MAKES 4 SERVINGS

1 tablespoon whole black peppercorns
1 teaspoon whole fennel seeds
4 beef tenderloin steaks (filet mignon), each 1 inch thick (about 4 ounces each)

3 medium peppers (red, yellow, and/or orange)
1 tablespoon minced fresh parsley
1 teaspoon olive oil
3/4 teaspoon salt

1. Prepare outdoor grill for covered direct grilling over medium-high heat.

2. Meanwhile, on cutting board, with rolling pin, crush peppercorns and fennel seeds. With hands, pat spice mixture around edges of steaks. Cover and refrigerate steaks until ready to cook. If you like, steaks can be prepared up to 1 day ahead.

3. Cut each pepper lengthwise in half; discard stems and seeds. With hand, flatten each pepper half.

4. Place peppers, skin side down, on hot grill rack. Cover grill and cook, until skins are charred and blistered, 8 to 10 minutes. Transfer peppers to bowl; cover with plate and let steam at room temperature until cool enough to handle, about 15 minutes. If using gas grill, reset temperature to medium.

5. Remove peppers from bowl. Peel skins and discard. Cut peppers lengthwise into 1/4-inch-wide strips. Return peppers to same bowl and toss with parsley, oil, and 1/4 teaspoon salt.

6. Sprinkle steaks with remaining 1/2 teaspoon salt. Place steaks on hot grill rack over medium heat. Cover grill and cook, turning once, 8 to 10 minutes for medium-rare or until desired doneness. Serve steaks topped with peppers.

Each serving: About 230 calories, 26g protein, 9g carbohydrate, 10g total fat (3g saturated), 71mg cholesterol, 495mg sodium.

Filet Mignon with Horseradish Salsa

Juicy steaks taste even better with our flavor-packed salsa. Looking for a new vegetable idea? Try grilling young onions right along with the meat. For an extra-special company dinner, grill portobello mushrooms as you would in Portobello and Prosciutto Salad (page 30) and serve thickly sliced mushrooms along with the meat and salsa.

PREP: 15 MINUTES   GRILL: 10 TO 12 MINUTES   MAKES 4 SERVINGS

Horseradish Salsa (page 229)
1 teaspoon cracked black
  pepper
1 teaspoon olive oil
1/2 teaspoon salt
1/4 teaspoon dried thyme

1 garlic clove, crushed with
  garlic press
4 beef tenderloin steaks (filet
  mignon), each 1 inch thick (about
  6 ounces each)

1. Prepare Horseradish Salsa.

2. Prepare outdoor grill for direct grilling over medium heat.

3. In cup, mix pepper, olive oil, salt, thyme, and garlic. Rub pepper mixture all over steaks.

4. Place steaks on hot grill rack over medium heat and grill, turning once, 10 to 12 minutes for medium-rare or until desired doneness. Serve steaks with Horseradish Salsa.

Each serving: About 330 calories, 39g protein, 9g carbohydrate, 15g total fat (4g saturated), 89mg cholesterol, 710mg sodium.

TIP: This pepper rub also works beautifully with flank steak, skirt steak, or any sirloin cut.

Filet Mignon with Horseradish Salsa

Red Wine-Marinated London Broil

The tasty herbed marinade not only adds flavor—it tenderizes the meat. Fresh rosemary will taste sensational, but if you can't find it use 2 teaspoons dried rosemary, crumbled.

PREP: 10 MINUTES PLUS MARINATING   GRILL: 12 TO 15 MINUTES
MAKES 8 SERVINGS

1/4 cup dry red wine

2 tablespoons soy sauce

2 tablespoons balsamic vinegar

2 tablespoons chopped fresh
  rosemary leaves

1 tablespoon tomato paste

1 tablespoon Dijon mustard

1/4 teaspoon crushed red pepper

4 large garlic cloves, crushed
  with press

1 beef top round steak (London
  broil), 1 inch thick (about 2
  pounds)

1. In small bowl, with wire whisk, mix wine, soy sauce, vinegar, rosemary, tomato paste, mustard, crushed red pepper, and garlic. Pour marinade into large ziptight plastic bag. Add steak to marinade, turning to coat. Seal bag, pressing out excess air. Place bag on plate; refrigerate steak, turning several times, 4 to 6 hours.
2. Prepare outdoor grill for covered direct grilling over medium heat.
3. Remove steak from bag; discard marinade. Place steak on hot grill rack over medium heat. Cover grill and cook steak, turning once, 12 to 15 minutes for medium-rare or until desired doneness. Transfer steak to cutting board and let stand 10 minutes to allow juices to set for easier slicing.
4. To serve, thinly slice steak on the diagonal across the grain. Arrange on platter.

Each serving: About 185 calories, 26g protein, 1g carbohydrate, 8g total fat (3g saturated), 72mg cholesterol, 115mg sodium.

Chili-Crusted Flank Steak

The combination of chili powder, sugar, and salt gives the beef a sweet and spicy crust. Grilled red onions, lightly charred and tender, would make a nice addition to any meal off the grill. Serve with Campfire Corn with Herb Butter (page 187) and grilled bread.

PREP: 10 MINUTES   GRILL: 15 TO 20 MINUTES   MAKES 6 SERVINGS

2 tablespoons chili powder
1 tablespoon brown sugar
1/4 teaspoon salt
2 tablespoons fresh lime juice
1 large garlic clove, crushed with garlic press

1 beef flank steak (about 1 1/2 pounds)
3 large red onions (about 8 ounces each), each cut into 6 wedges
1 tablespoon olive oil

1. Prepare outdoor grill for direct grilling over medium heat.

2. In cup, mix chili powder, brown sugar, salt, lime juice, and garlic. Rub chili-powder mixture on both sides of steak. In medium bowl, toss red onions with olive oil.

3. Place steak and onions on hot grill rack over medium heat. Grill steak, turning once, 15 to 20 minutes for medium-rare or until desired doneness. Cook onions, turning occasionally, until browned and just tender, about 15 minutes.

4. Transfer onions and steak to cutting board. Let steak stand 10 minutes to allow juices to set for easier slicing. Thinly slice steak and serve with grilled onions.

Each serving: About 270 calories, 24g protein, 15g carbohydrate, 13g total fat (5g saturated), 57mg cholesterol, 200mg sodium.

TIP: You can soak wooden skewers in water for 15 minutes, then thread the onion wedges onto the skewers; the wedges won't separate and will be easier to handle.

Pastrami-Spiced Flank Steak

Pastrami-Spiced Flank Steak

Pastrami, a popular New York City deli item, probably came to us via the Romanians, who prepared many of their meats by smoking. Although our pastrami isn't smoked, it is similarly coated with coarse pepper and other aromatic spices. Serve it on sliced rye with a side of coleslaw, deli style!

PREP: 15 MINUTES PLUS MARINATING   GRILL: 13 TO 15 MINUTES
MAKES 6 SERVINGS

1 tablespoon coriander seeds
1 tablespoon paprika
1 tablespoon cracked black pepper
2 teaspoons ground ginger
1 1/2 teaspoons salt
1 teaspoon sugar
1/2 teaspoon crushed red pepper

3 garlic cloves, crushed with
  garlic press
1 beef flank steak (about
  1 1/2 pounds)
12 slices rye bread
deli-style mustard

1. In mortar with pestle or in ziptight plastic bag with rolling pin, crush coriander seeds. In cup, mix coriander, paprika, black pepper, ginger, salt, sugar, and crushed red pepper.
2. Rub garlic on both sides of steak, then pat with spice mixture. Place steak in large ziptight plastic bag; seal bag, pressing out excess air. Place bag on plate; refrigerate at least 2 hours, or up to 24 hours.
3. Prepare outdoor grill for direct grilling over medium heat.
4. Remove steak from bag. Place steak on hot grill rack over medium heat and grill, turning once, 13 to 15 minutes for medium-rare or until desired doneness.
5. Place bread slices on grill rack over medium heat and toast, without turning, just until grill marks appear on underside of bread.
6. Transfer steak to cutting board. Let stand 10 minutes to allow juices to set for easier slicing. Thinly slice steak across the grain and serve with grilled rye bread and mustard.

Each serving: About 380 calories, 33g protein, 35g carbohydrate, 12g total fat (4g saturated), 47mg cholesterol, 1,015mg sodium.

TIP: Grinding whole spices in a mortar with a pestle releases their flavorful oils, which makes the steak even tastier.

Korean Steak

Set out bowls of crisp romaine lettuce, rice, green onions, and sesame seeds and let each person assemble his or her own package.

PREP: 40 MINUTES PLUS MARINATING   GRILL: 14 TO 15 MINUTES
MAKES 6 SERVINGS

1/2 cup reduced-sodium soy sauce

2 tablespoons sugar

2 tablespoons minced, peeled fresh ginger

2 tablespoons seasoned rice vinegar

1 tablespoon Asian sesame oil

1/4 teaspoon ground red pepper (cayenne)

3 garlic cloves, pressed

1 1/2 pounds beef top round or sirloin steak, 1 inch thick

1 cup regular long-grain rice

3 green onions, thinly sliced

1 tablespoon sesame seeds, toasted

1 head romaine lettuce, separated into leaves

1. In large ziptight plastic bag, combine soy sauce, sugar, ginger, vinegar, sesame oil, ground red pepper, and garlic; add steak, turning to coat. Seal bag, pressing out excess air. Place on plate; refrigerate steak 1 to 4 hours to marinate, turning once.

2. Prepare outdoor grill for direct grilling over medium heat.

3. Just before grilling steak, prepare rice; keep warm.

4. Remove steak from bag; reserve marinade. Place steak on hot grill rack over medium heat and grill, turning once, 14 to 15 minutes for medium-rare or until desired doneness. Transfer steak to cutting board; let stand 10 minutes to allow juices to set for easier slicing.

5. In 1-quart saucepan, heat reserved marinade and *1/4 cup water* to boiling over high heat; boil 2 minutes.

6. To serve, thinly slice steak. Let each person place some steak slices, rice, green onions, and sesame seeds on a lettuce leaf, then drizzle with some cooked marinade. Fold sides of lettuce leaf over filling to form a packet to eat like a sandwich.

Each serving: About 370 calories, 30g protein, 35g carbohydrate, 11g total fat (3g saturated), 69mg cholesterol, 960mg sodium.

TIP: Toasting brings out the nutty flavor of sesame seeds. To toast, heat seeds in a small, dry skillet over moderate heat, stirring constantly, until fragrant and a shade darker.

Coffee-and-Spice Steak with Cool Salsa

A dry rub of instant coffee, cinnamon, and allspice adds a rich, roasted, caramelized flavor. Our crisp watermelon and cucumber salsa is a refreshing go-along with any meat.

PREP: 30 MINUTES   GRILL: 12 TO 15 MINUTES   MAKES 6 SERVINGS

COOL SALSA
- 1 lime
- 2 cups 1/4-inch cubes watermelon
- 1/2 English (seedless) cucumber, unpeeled and cut into 1/4-inch cubes
- 1 green onion, minced
- 1/4 teaspoon salt
- 1/8 teaspoon coarsely ground black pepper

COFFEE-AND-SPICE STEAK
- 2 teaspoons instant-coffee granules
- 1 teaspoon sugar
- 1 teaspoon salt
- 1 teaspoon coarsely ground black pepper
- 1/2 teaspoon ground cinnamon
- 1/4 teaspoon ground allspice
- 1 beef flank steak (about 1 1/2 pounds)
- 2 teaspoons olive oil

1. Prepare salsa: From lime, grate 1 teaspoon peel and squeeze 2 tablespoons juice. In medium bowl, toss lime peel and juice with watermelon, cucumber, green onion, salt, and pepper. Cover and refrigerate salsa up to 2 hours if not serving right away. Makes about 3 1/2 cups.

2. Prepare outdoor grill for direct grilling over medium heat.

3. Prepare steak: In cup, mix coffee granules, sugar, salt, pepper, cinnamon, and allspice. Coat both sides of steak with oil, then rub with coffee mixture.

4. Place steak on hot grill rack over medium heat and grill, turning once, 12 to 15 minutes for medium-rare or until desired doneness.

5. Transfer steak to cutting board; let stand 10 minutes to allow juices to set for easier slicing. Thinly slice steak and serve with salsa.

Each serving: About 215 calories, 27g protein, 1g carbohydrate, 11g total fat (4g saturated), 47mg cholesterol, 445mg sodium.

Each 1/4 cup salsa: About 20 calories, 0g protein, 4g carbohydrate, 0g total fat (0g saturated), 0mg cholesterol, 80mg sodium.

Anise Beef Kabobs

We like to buy a sirloin steak and cut it into chunks to ensure equal-size pieces for even grilling. But, if you prefer, use precut beef cubes from your supermarket for the kabobs. The rub and meat can easily be doubled to feed a larger crowd. Serve with bowls of rice.

PREP: 10 MINUTES PLUS STANDING   GRILL: 8 TO 10 MINUTES
MAKES 4 SERVINGS

1 teaspoon anise seeds or fennel seeds
2 teaspoons olive oil
1/2 teaspoon salt
1/4 teaspoon coarsely ground black pepper

pinch crushed red pepper (optional)
1 boneless beef top sirloin steak, 1 inch thick (1 pound) cut into 1 1/4-inch chunks
4 (8-inch) metal skewers

1. Prepare outdoor grill for direct grilling over medium heat.

2. In mortar with pestle or in ziptight plastic bag with rolling pin, crush anise seeds. In medium bowl, combine anise seeds, oil, salt, coarsely ground black pepper, and crushed red pepper, if using. Add beef chunks, tossing until well coated. Cover and let beef stand 10 minutes at room temperature to marinate.

3. Loosely thread meat onto skewers. Place skewers on hot grill rack over medium heat; grill, turning occasionally, 8 to 10 minutes for medium-rare or until desired doneness.

Each serving: About 220 calories, 21g protein, 0g carbohydrate, 14g total fat (5g saturated), 68mg cholesterol, 340mg sodium.

TIP: If you like, toss chunks of onion and peppers in a tablespoon of olive oil and thread onto the skewers along with the meat.

Anise Beef Kabobs

Korean-Style Sesame Short Ribs

Marinating overnight makes these meaty ribs irresistible. Serve with a spicy cabbage slaw, a cool rice salad, and Glazed Japanese Eggplant (page 195). If you like, sprinkle the short ribs with sesame seeds and thinly sliced green onion just before serving.

PREP: 15 MINUTES PLUS OVERNIGHT TO MARINATE
GRILL: 20 TO 25 MINUTES   MAKES 6 SERVINGS

4 pounds beef chuck short ribs, cut into 2-inch pieces
1/2 cup reduced-sodium soy sauce
4 teaspoons minced, peeled fresh ginger

2 teaspoons Asian sesame oil
3 large garlic cloves, minced

1. With sharp knife, cut 1/4-inch deep slashes in meaty side of short ribs at 1/2-inch intervals.

2. In ziptight plastic bag, combine soy sauce, ginger, sesame oil, and garlic. Add short ribs, turning to coat. Seal bag, pressing out as much air as possible. Place bag in 13" by 9" baking dish and refrigerate overnight to marinate, turning once.

3. Prepare outdoor grill for direct grilling over medium heat.

4. Lift ribs from bag, reserving marinade. Place ribs on hot grill rack over medium heat and brush with remaining marinade. Grill, turning ribs occasionally, 20 to 25 minutes for medium-rare or until desired doneness.

Each serving: About 745 calories, 34g protein, 3g carbohydrate, 65g total fat (27g saturated), 142mg cholesterol, 880mg sodium.

TIP: Golden brown (roasted), nutty-tasting sesame oil is a flavoring oil as opposed to a cooking oil. Use a little sesame oil to add flavor to stir-fries and Asian noodle dishes.

Steak Fajitas with Guacamole

Spicy skirt steak with onions makes a memorable Tex-Mex meal. A typical piece of skirt steak is long, about 4 inches wide, and $1/2$ inch thick. If you can't find any skirt steak, flank steak is a good alternative. If low-fat flour tortillas are not available, substitute regular tortillas.

PREP: 25 MINUTES   GRILL: 20 MINUTES   MAKES 8 SERVINGS

Guacamole (page 222)
3 tablespoons chili powder
1 teaspoon ground cumin
$1/2$ teaspoon salt
$1/4$ teaspoon ground red pepper
   (cayenne)
1 beef skirt steak or flank steak
   (1 $3/4$ pounds)

2 large red onions (12 ounces each),
   sliced
1 tablespoon olive oil
8 (12-inch) low-fat flour tortillas
lime wedges
sour cream

1. Prepare guacamole. In cup, mix chili powder, cumin, salt, and ground red pepper. Rub steak with 2 tablespoons chili-powder mixture; set aside.
2. Prepare outdoor grill for direct grilling over medium heat.
3. In large bowl, toss onions with oil and remaining chili-powder mixture until well coated. Layer two 24" by 18" sheets heavy-duty foil for double thickness. Place onion mixture in center of foil. Bring short ends of foil up and over onions, and fold several times to seal. Fold remaining sides of foil several times to seal in juices.
4. Place foil packet on grill over medium heat. Cook onions, turning the packet over halfway through cooking, until onions are tender, about 20 minutes.
5. Place steak on grill rack with onions; grill steak, turning once, 10 to 15 minutes, depending on thickness, for medium or until desired doneness. Transfer steak to cutting board; let stand 10 minutes to allow juices to set for easier slicing. Transfer onions to bowl; cover and keep warm.
6. Wrap tortillas in foil; place near edge of grill over low heat until warm.
7. To serve, thinly slice steak. Place steak and onions on warm tortillas; top with some guacamole and roll up to eat. Serve with lime wedges, sour cream, and remaining guacamole.

Each serving: About 485 calories, 29g protein, 52g carbohydrate, 18g total fat (5g saturated), 49mg cholesterol, 925mg sodium.

Jerk Steak Kabobs
with Pineapple Salsa

Jerk Steak Kabobs with Pineapple Salsa

The hot Caribbean coating on the meat is the perfect foil for our cool tropical salsa. Allspice, a berry grown in the Caribbean, has the combined flavors of cinnamon, cloves, and nutmeg. It is available whole or ground; you'll find it on the spice shelf in your supermarket.

PREP: 30 MINUTES PLUS STANDING   GRILL: 8 TO 10 MINUTES
MAKES 4 SERVINGS

Pineapple Salsa (page 223)
2 green onions, minced
2 tablespoons lime juice
2 tablespoons brown sugar
1 tablespoon Worcestershire sauce
1 tablespoon grated, peeled fresh ginger
1 teaspoon vegetable oil
1 teaspoon salt
1 teaspoon dried thyme
1 teaspoon ground allspice
1/2 teaspoon ground red pepper (cayenne)
1 boneless beef top sirloin steak, 1 1/4 inches thick (1 1/2 pounds), cut into 1 1/4-inch cubes
4 (12-inch) metal skewers

1. Prepare Pineapple Salsa, cover, and refrigerate.
2. Prepare outdoor grill for direct grilling over medium heat.
3. Meanwhile, in large bowl, mix green onions, lime juice, brown sugar, Worcestershire, ginger, oil, salt, thyme, allspice, and ground red pepper. Add steak cubes and toss to coat well; let stand 15 minutes at room temperature to marinate.
4. Thread steak cubes onto skewers. Place skewers on hot grill rack over medium heat; grill, turning occasionally, 8 to 10 minutes for medium-rare. Serve kabobs with salsa.

Each serving: About 375 calories, 34g protein, 30g carbohydrate, 13g total fat (5g saturated), 102mg cholesterol, 790mg sodium.

Steak Sandwiches with Grilled Onions

Marinating the steak with a delicious blend of Asian flavors and grilling it takes this classic sandwich to a new level.

PREP: 15 MINUTES PLUS MARINATING   GRILL: 12 TO 15 MINUTES
MAKES 4 SERVINGS

1/4 cup soy sauce
1/4 cup balsamic vinegar
1 tablespoon brown sugar
1 tablespoon fresh thyme leaves
1/4 teaspoon ground black pepper
1 beef flank steak (about 1 1/4 pounds)
1 (12-inch) metal skewer

1 medium red onion (about 8 ounces), cut into 4 thick slices
8 slices sourdough bread, toasted on grill, if you like
2 ripe medium tomatoes, sliced
1 bunch arugula, tough stems discarded

1. In large ziptight plastic bag, mix soy sauce, vinegar, sugar, thyme, and pepper. Add steak, turning to coat. Seal bag, pressing out excess air. Place bag on plate; let stand 15 minutes at room temperature or 1 hour in the refrigerator, turning several times.

2. Prepare outdoor grill for covered direct grilling over medium heat.

3. Meanwhile, for easier handling, insert metal skewer horizontally through onion slices; set aside.

4. Remove steak from marinade; pour marinade into 1-quart saucepan. Heat marinade over high heat to boiling; boil 2 minutes.

5. Place steak and onion slices on hot grill rack. Cover grill and cook steak and onions, brushing both with marinade occasionally and turning both over once, until onions are browned and tender and meat is medium-rare, 12 to 15 minutes. Transfer steak to cutting board; separate onion into rings.

6. Thinly slice steak diagonally across grain. Arrange onion rings and steak on 4 slices of bread; spoon any meat juices from board over onion and steak. Top with tomatoes, arugula, and remaining 4 slices of bread.

Each serving: About 210 calories, 9g protein, 38g carbohydrate, 3g total fat (1g saturated), 5mg cholesterol, 815mg sodium.

Steak Sandwiches
with Grilled Onions

The Perfect Burger

(pictured on front cover)

Our take on a classic makes this burger an instant hit. Serve burgers on buns with lettuce, tomato, and onion.

PREP 10 MINUTES GRILL ABOUT 8 MINUTES MAKES 4 MAIN-DISH SERVINGS

4 (12-inch) bamboo skewers
1 1/4 pounds ground beef chuck
1/2 teaspoon coarsely ground black
  pepper
1 teaspoon salt

1 large sweet onion such as Vidalia
  or Maui, cut into 1/2-inch rounds
4 hamburger buns, split
2 ripe medium tomatoes, thinly
  sliced

1. Soak skewers in water to cover 15 minutes. Meanwhile, prepare outdoor grill for direct grilling over medium heat, or preheat ridged grill pan over medium heat until very hot.

2. Shape ground beef into 4 patties. Sprinkle pepper and ¾ teaspoon salt on both sides of patties. Thread 1 skewer horizontally through center of each onion slice. Sprinkle onion with remaining salt.

3. Place burgers and onion slices on hot grill rack; cook 8 to 10 minutes, turning over once. Burgers should have an internal temperature of 160°F. Onions should be browned and tender. About 1 minute before burgers are done, add buns, cut sides down, to grill rack. Grill just until toasted.

Each serving: About 485 calories, 31 g protein, 33 g carbohydrates, 25 g total fat (9 g saturated), 4 g fiber, 96 mg cholesterol, 920 mg sodium.

THE STEPS

1. Divide meat into 4 equal portions; shape each into a ¾-inch thick patty. Handle as little as possible so burgers won't be tough.

2. Cook thoroughly. To test doneness, insert instant-read thermometer horizontally into center of each burger.

Greek Burgers

Place the pitas on the grill to toast just before the burgers come off the grill. If you'd like, add crumbled feta cheese and chopped ripe tomatoes to the pitas before serving. Serve the burgers with a crisp romaine lettuce salad tossed with a lemony vinaigrette and snipped fresh dill.

PREP: 5 MINUTES   GRILL: 10 TO 12 MINUTES   MAKES 4 SERVINGS

1 pound lean ground beef (90%)
1/4 cup chopped fresh parsley
1 teaspoon dried mint, crumbled
1/2 teaspoon salt

1/4 teaspoon coarsely ground
   black pepper
4 (6-inch) pitas

1. Prepare outdoor grill for direct grilling over medium heat.

2. In medium bowl, combine ground beef, parsley, mint, salt, and pepper just until well blended but not overmixed. Shape mixture into 4 patties, each 1 inch thick, handling meat as little as possible. (Gentle handling is one of the keys to juicy burgers. Use a light hand when shaping patties, so burgers won't come out compact and dry.)

3. Place burgers on hot grill rack over medium heat and grill, turning once, 10 to 12 minutes for medium or until desired doneness.

4. Meanwhile, cut off 1 inch across top of each pita. Serve burgers in pitas.

Each serving: About 360 calories, 29g protein, 34g carbohydrate, 12g total fat (5g saturated), 70mg cholesterol, 695mg sodium.

TIP: Before shaping plain burgers, tuck a chunk of soft, melting cheese such as Fontina, Cheddar, or Roquefort into the center and shape the patty around it to make an inside-out cheeseburger.

Tex-Mex Burgers

Tex-Mex Burgers

For an all-out splurge, serve burgers with shredded lettuce, sliced red onion, extra salsa, and a topping of Guacamole (page 222). For a spicier burger, choose a medium to hot salsa and increase the chili powder to 2 teaspoons. Top the burger with sliced Monterey Jack, cover grill to melt the cheese, and you've got a Tex-Mex cheeseburger.

PREP: 5 MINUTES   GRILL: 10 TO 12 MINUTES   MAKES 4 SERVINGS

1 pound lean ground beef (90%)	1/2 teaspoon salt
2 tablespoons minced onion	1 teaspoon chili powder
2 tablespoons bottled salsa	4 seeded rolls, split

1. Prepare outdoor grill for direct grilling over medium heat.

2. In medium bowl, combine ground beef, onion, salsa, salt, and chili powder just until well blended but not overmixed. Shape mixture into 4 patties, each 1 inch thick, handling meat as little as possible. (Gentle handling is one of the keys to juicy burgers. Use a light hand when shaping patties, so burgers won't come out compact and dry.)

3. Place burgers on hot grill rack over medium heat and grill, turning once, 10 to 12 minutes for medium or until desired doneness.

4. Place rolls, cut side down, on grill over medium heat and toast, without turning, just until grill marks appear on cut side of rolls. Serve burgers on rolls.

Each serving: About 325 calories, 27g protein, 23g carbohydrate, 14 g total fat (5g saturated), 70mg cholesterol, 670mg sodium.

TIP: The best ground beef for burgers has some fat in it (about 10% works nicely) for juiciness and flavor, so don't use the leanest ground beef.

Stuffed Veal Chops

Thick, juicy veal chops, stuffed with a mixture of creamy cheese, roasted peppers, and basil, sit atop a bed of spicy greens. The combination of warm chop and cool greens is a real winner. Use a small paring knife to cut the pocket so that it is deep but not wide.

PREP: 15 MINUTES   GRILL: 10 TO 12 MINUTES   MAKES 4 SERVINGS

1/4 cup roasted red peppers (one-third 7-ounce jar), drained and chopped
3 tablespoons chopped fresh basil
4 veal rib chops, each 1 inch thick (about 10 ounces each)
2 ounces Fontina cheese, sliced
1/2 plus 1/8 teaspoon salt

1/2 plus 1/8 teaspoon coarsely ground black pepper
1 tablespoon olive oil
1 tablespoon balsamic vinegar
1/2 teaspoon Dijon mustard
4 ounces arugula, watercress, or baby spinach, tough stems removed

1. Prepare outdoor grill for direct grilling over medium-high heat.
2. In small bowl, mix roasted red peppers and 2 tablespoons chopped basil.
3. Prepare veal chops: Holding knife parallel to surface, cut a horizontal pocket in each chop. Tuck cheese slices into veal pockets; spread red-pepper mixture over cheese. Sprinkle veal chops with 1/2 teaspoon salt and 1/2 teaspoon pepper.
4. Place chops on hot grill rack over medium-high heat and grill, turning chops once, until chops are lightly browned on both sides and just lose their pink color throughout, 10 to 12 minutes.
5. Prepare arugula salad: In medium bowl, with wire whisk, mix oil, vinegar, remaining 1 tablespoon basil, mustard, remaining 1/8 teaspoon salt, and remaining 1/8 teaspoon pepper; add arugula, tossing to coat.
6. To serve, spoon arugula mixture onto platter; arrange chops on top.

Each serving: About 440 calories, 40g protein, 2g carbohydrate, 29g total fat (11g saturated), 181mg cholesterol, 655mg sodium.

Stuffed Veal Chops

Kansas City Ribs

Baby back ribs with a gooey tomato-based sauce are a summer tradition.

PREP: 1 HOUR 15 MINUTES   GRILL: 13 TO 20 MINUTES
MAKES 6 SERVINGS

RIBS
- 3 racks pork baby back ribs (about 1 pound each)
- 1 onion, cut into quarters
- 1 orange, cut into quarters
- 1 tablespoon whole black peppercorns
- 1 tablespoon whole coriander seeds

BARBECUE SAUCE
- 3 tablespoons butter or margarine
- 1 medium onion, chopped
- 4 garlic cloves, chopped
- 1 can (15 ounces) tomato sauce
- 1/4 cup cider vinegar
- 1/4 cup packed brown sugar
- 1 teaspoon salt
- 1/4 teaspoon coarsely ground black pepper

1. Prepare ribs: In 8-quart saucepot, place ribs, onion, orange, pepper-corns, and coriander seeds. Add enough *water to cover*; heat to boiling over high heat. Reduce heat to low; partially cover and cook until ribs are fork-tender, 50 minutes to 1 hour. Transfer ribs to platter. If not serving right away, cover and refrigerate until ready to serve.

2. Meanwhile, prepare barbecue sauce: In 2-quart saucepan, heat butter over medium heat until melted. Add onion and garlic and cook, stirring occasionally, until softened, about 8 minutes. Add tomato sauce, vinegar, sugar, salt, and pepper; heat to boiling over high heat. Reduce heat to low; simmer, stirring occasionally, until thickened, 40 minutes. Makes about 2 2/3 cups.

3. Prepare outdoor grill for covered direct grilling over medium heat.

4. Place ribs on hot grill rack over medium heat. Cover grill and cook ribs, turning once, until browned, 8 to 10 minutes. Brush ribs with sauce and cook, brushing with remaining sauce and turning frequently, 5 to 10 minutes longer.

5. To serve, cut racks into 1-rib portions and arrange on platter.

Each serving: About 380 calories, 24g protein, 9g carbohydrate, 27g total fat (12g saturated), 74mg cholesterol, 520mg sodium.

Plum-Good Baby Back Ribs

Licorice-flavored star anise—one of the spices in Chinese five-spice pow-der—gives these ribs their distinctive appeal. The ribs can be cooked in the seasoned liquid up to two days ahead, then cooled, covered, and re-frigerated. Remove the ribs from the refrigerator while the grill heats, then proceed with the recipe.

PREP: 1 HOUR   GRILL: 15 TO 20 MINUTES   MAKES 6 SERVINGS

4 racks pork baby back ribs
  (about 1 pound each)
12 whole black peppercorns
2 bay leaves
10 whole star anise
2 cinnamon sticks (each 3 inches long)

1/4 cup soy sauce
1 jar (12 ounces) plum jam (1 cup)
1 tablespoon grated, peeled fresh ginger
1 garlic clove, crushed with garlic press

1. In 8-quart saucepot, heat ribs, peppercorns, bay leaves, 4 star anise, and 1 cinnamon stick. Add enough *water to cover*, heat to boiling over high heat. Reduce heat to low; cover and simmer until ribs are fork-tender, 50 min-utes to 1 hour. Transfer ribs to platter. If not serving right away, cover and refrigerate until ready to serve.

2. Prepare glaze: In 1-quart saucepan, heat soy sauce, remaining 6 star anise and 1 cinnamon stick to boiling over high heat. Reduce heat to low; cover and simmer 5 minutes. Remove from heat; let stand, covered, 5 minutes. Strain mixture into bowl; discard star anise and cinnamon. Stir in plum jam, ginger, and garlic.

3. Prepare outdoor grill for direct grilling over medium heat.

4. Place ribs on hot grill rack over medium heat; grill, turning once, until browned, 10 minutes. Brush ribs with some glaze and grill, brushing with remaining glaze and turning frequently, 5 to 10 minutes longer.

Each serving: About 690 calories, 37g protein, 38g carbohydrate, 43g total fat (16g saturated), 172mg cholesterol, 860mg sodium.

Ribs Supreme

Only fifteen minutes of grilling time! The trick: Steam the seasoned ribs for an hour in the oven up to two days before barbecuing. With both the ribs and the BBQ sauce prepared in advance, this could easily become a part of your summer weeknight repertoire.

PREP: 1 HOUR 15 MINUTES   GRILL: 15 MINUTES   MAKES 6 SERVINGS

4 teaspoons grated, peeled fresh ginger
2 teaspoons grated fresh lemon peel
3/4 teaspoon salt
2 garlic cloves, crushed with garlic press

4 racks pork baby back ribs (about 1 pound each)
2 cups Secret-Recipe BBQ Sauce (page 220)

1. Preheat oven to 350°F. In cup, mix ginger, lemon peel, salt, and garlic until combined. Rub ginger mixture on ribs.

2. Place ribs in large roasting pan (15 1/2" by 11 1/2"), overlapping slightly. Pour *2 cups boiling water* into roasting pan. Cover pan tightly with foil and place in oven. Steam ribs 1 hour.

3. Meanwhile, prepare Secret-Recipe BBQ Sauce.

4. Carefully remove foil from roasting pan (escaping steam is very hot). Remove ribs from pan; discard water. Ribs may be grilled immediately or refrigerated up to 2 days before grilling.

5. Prepare outdoor grill for direct grilling over medium heat.

6. Place ribs, meat side up, on hot grill rack over medium heat; grill, turning once, 5 minutes. Turn ribs over; brush with BBQ sauce and grill 5 minutes. Turn ribs over again; brush with more sauce and grill 5 minutes longer. Cut racks into 2-rib portions; serve with remaining sauce.

Each serving: About 615 calories, 36g protein, 16g carbohydrate, 44g total fat (16g saturated), 172mg cholesterol, 760mg sodium.

TIP: When buying baby backs, look for ribs that are meaty, with a minimum of visible fat.

Ribs Supreme

Jerk Pork Tenderloins

Jerk Pork Tenderloins

From Jamaica, jerk seasoning uses lots of allspice, which is native to the island. Combined with thyme, bay leaves, and hot chiles, it makes a unique and delicious rub for pork.

PREP: 15 MINUTES PLUS MARINATING   GRILL: 18 TO 22 MINUTES
MAKES 8 SERVINGS

1 bunch green onions, cut into 1-inch pieces
3 bay leaves, broken into pieces
3 garlic cloves, peeled
2 jalapeño chiles, seeds and membrane discarded, coarsely chopped
2 tablespoons distilled white vinegar
1 tablespoon dried thyme
2 teaspoons ground allspice
1 teaspoon salt
1/2 teaspoon coarsely ground black pepper
2 whole pork tenderloins (1 pound each)
2 small or 1 large ripe pineapple

1. In food processor with knife blade attached, puree green onions, bay leaves, garlic, jalapeños, vinegar, thyme, allspice, salt, and pepper to a thick paste.

2. On large plate, rub jerk paste on tenderloins; cover and refrigerate 1 hour or overnight.

3. Prepare outdoor grill for covered direct grilling over medium heat.

4. Meanwhile, with sharp knife, cut pineapple lengthwise through crown to stem end into 8 wedges, leaving on leafy crown.

5. Place tenderloins on hot grill rack over medium heat. Cover grill and cook, turning tenderloins once, until browned on the outside and still slightly pink in the center, 18 to 22 minutes. Meat thermometer inserted in thickest part of tenderloin should register 155°F.

6. While tenderloins are cooking, add pineapple wedges, cut sides down, to same grill rack; cook, turning once, until golden brown and heated through, 5 to 8 minutes.

7. Transfer pineapple to platter. Transfer tenderloin to cutting board and thinly slice. Serve sliced tenderloins with pineapple wedges.

Each serving: About 205 calories, 27g protein, 10g carbohydrate, 6g total fat (2g saturated), 78mg cholesterol, 340mg sodium.

Spiced Pork Tenderloin with Mango Salsa

A simple blend of warm spices lends exotic flavor to lean and tender pork "cutlets." The salsa adds a tropical taste. Prepare the salsa several hours in advance, rub the pork with the spice mixture, and let it marinate while the grill heats up, then cook dinner in a matter of minutes.

PREP: 20 MINUTES   GRILL: 6 TO 7 MINUTES   MAKES 8 SERVINGS

Mango Salsa (page 224)
2 pork tenderloins (about 1 pound each), trimmed
3 tablespoons all-purpose flour
1 teaspoon salt
1 teaspoon ground cumin
1 teaspoon ground coriander
1/2 teaspoon ground cinnamon
1/2 teaspoon ground ginger

1. Prepare Mango Salsa; cover and refrigerate.
2. Prepare outdoor grill for direct grilling over medium heat.
3. Cut each pork tenderloin lengthwise almost in half, being careful not to cut all the way through. Open and spread flat. Place each tenderloin between two sheets of plastic wrap; with meat mallet or rolling pin, pound to 1/4-inch thickness. Cut each tenderloin into 4 pieces.
4. On waxed paper, mix flour, salt, cumin, coriander, cinnamon, and ginger; use to coat pork.
5. Place pork on hot grill rack over medium heat and grill, turning once, until lightly browned on both sides and pork just loses its pink color throughout, 6 to 7 minutes. Serve with Mango Salsa.

Each serving: About 215 calories, 23g protein, 15g carbohydrate, 6g total fat (2g saturated), 71mg cholesterol, 455mg sodium.

Lime Pork Tenderloin
with Grilled Plums

For an easy all-on-the grill supper, serve this succulent pork with our short-cut sweet potatoes (see Tip below).

PREP: 30 MINUTES   GRILL 12 TO 15 MINUTES   MAKES 4 SERVINGS

1 whole pork tenderloin (about
  1 1/4 pounds)
1 large lime
1 teaspoon coarsely ground black
  pepper

1/2 teaspoon salt
4 large plums (about 1 1/4 pounds),
  each cut in half and pitted
1 tablespoon honey
pinch ground cloves

1. Prepare outdoor grill for covered direct grilling over medium heat.

2. Meanwhile, cut pork lengthwise in half. From lime, grate 1 teaspoon peel and squeeze 2 tablespoons juice. In cup, stir lime peel, pepper, and salt; rub mixture on pork. Spray pork with nonstick cooking spray.

3. Place pork on hot grill rack over medium heat. Cover grill and cook, turning over once, until browned on the outside and still slightly pink in the center, 12 to 15 minutes. After grilling pork 2 to 3 minutes, add plums; grill, turning over once, until browned, 10 minutes.

4. Transfer pork and plums to cutting board. Cut plums into wedges and place in bowl. Add honey, cloves, and lime juice; toss until coasted. Slice pork; serve with plum mixture.

Each serving: About 289 calories, 30g protein, 23g carbohydrate, 9g total fat (3g saturated), 90mg cholesterol, 351mg sodium.

TIP: As an accompaniment to the pork try short-cut grilled sweet potatoes: Cut *2 medium sweet potatoes* into 1/2-inch slices. Spray both sides with *nonstick cooking spray*; then sprinkle with 1/2 teaspoon salt. Place potatoes on microwave-safe plate. Cook in microwave oven on High 5 minutes. Transfer potatoes to hot grill rack and cook, covered, until brown on both sides, about 10 minutes.

Cuban Pork and Plantains with Black-Bean Salsa

Rub the meat with a peppery garlic coating and grill with plantains for a savory splurge. Make sure the plantains are very ripe: the skin should be black, and the fruit should yield to gentle pressure. (To speed ripening, place in a brown paper bag with a lime.)

PREP: 45 MINUTES   GRILL: 18 TO 20 MINUTES   MAKES 6 SERVINGS

BLACK-BEAN SALSA
- 2 limes
- 1 orange
- 1 can (15 to 19 ounces) black beans, rinsed and drained
- 1/2 small sweet onion, diced
- 1/4 cup loosely packed fresh cilantro leaves, chopped
- 1 medium jalapeño chile, seeded and minced
- 3/4 teaspoon salt

PORK AND PLANTAINS
- 2 large garlic cloves, crushed with garlic press
- 1 teaspoon salt
- 1 1/2 teaspoons coarsely ground black pepper
- 2 tablespoons olive oil
- 2 whole pork tenderloins (about 12 ounces each), trimmed
- 3 ripe medium plantains (about 1 1/2 pounds), peeled and each cut lengthwise in half

1. Prepare salsa: From limes, grate 1/2 teaspoon peel and squeeze 3 tablespoons juice. From orange, grate 1/2 teaspoon peel. With knife, remove remaining peel and white pith from orange and cut sections into 1/2-inch chunks. In medium bowl, combine lime peel and juice, orange peel, orange chunks, black beans, onion, cilantro, jalapeño, and salt. Cover and refrigerate salsa up to 2 days if not serving right away. Makes about 3 cups.

2. Prepare outdoor grill for direct grilling over medium heat.

3. Prepare pork and plantains: In cup, mix garlic, salt, pepper, and 1 tablespoon olive oil until blended. Rub garlic mixture on tenderloins. Brush plantains with remaining 1 tablespoon oil.

4. Place tenderloins on hot grill rack over medium heat and grill, turning once, until browned on the outside and still slightly pink in the center, and meat thermometer inserted in center of pork reaches 155°F, 18 to 20 minutes. Place plantains on same grill rack and cook, turning once, until tender and browned, 7 to 8 minutes.

5. Transfer plantains to platter. Transfer tenderloins to cutting board and thinly slice. Serve sliced tenderloins and plantains with Black–Bean Salsa.

Each serving pork and plantains: About 315 calories, 28g protein, 29g carbohydrate, 11g total fat (3g saturated), 78mg cholesterol, 440mg sodium.

Each 1/2 cup salsa: About 70 calories, 4g protein, 17g carbohydrate, 0g total fat (0g saturated), 0mg cholesterol, 475mg sodium.

Pork Tenderloins with Oregano

A lemon-herb marinade gives this lean cut of pork a zippy flavor. Twenty minutes is all it needs; the lemon juice will start to break down the meat fibers if it marinates much longer. To complete the dinner, serve with Grilled Vegetables Vinaigrette (page 204).

PREP: 10 MINUTES PLUS MARINATING   GRILL: ABOUT 20 MINUTES
MAKES 6 SERVINGS

1/4 cup fresh lemon juice
2 tablespoons chopped fresh oregano
  or 1 teaspoon dried oregano
2 tablespoons chopped fresh parsley
2 pork tenderloins (about 12 ounces
  each), trimmed

1 tablespoon olive oil
1/2 teaspoon salt
1/4 teaspoon coarsely ground
  black pepper

1. In large ziptight plastic bag, combine lemon juice and 1 tablespoon each oregano and parsley. Add tenderloins, turning to coat. Seal bag, pressing out excess air. Place bag on plate; refrigerate tenderloins 20 minutes to marinate, turning once.

2. Prepare outdoor grill for direct grilling over medium heat.

3. Remove tenderloins from bag; discard marinade. In cup, mix oil, salt, pepper, and remaining 1 tablespoon each oregano and parsley; rub mixture on tenderloins.

4. Place tenderloins on hot grill rack over medium heat and grill, turning occasionally, until browned on the outside and still slightly pink in the center, and meat thermometer inserted in center of pork reaches 155°F, about 20 minutes.

5. When tenderloins are done, transfer to warm large platter and let stand 5 minutes to set juices for easier slicing. Thinly slice tenderloins to serve.

Each serving: About 175 calories, 23g protein, 1g carbohydrate, 8g total fat (3g saturated), 71mg cholesterol, 240mg sodium.

TIP: To prevent bacterial contamination from raw meat, always follow the "two-platter" rule: Use one platter for transporting meat, poultry, or fish to the grill, then use a second, clean one for the cooked food.

Southern Peach Pork Chops

Juicy July peaches hot off the grill are perfect with tender, seared meat. If you'd like more of a kick from the curry rub, try using Madras curry powder; it is somewhat hotter than regular curry powder. Lightly brush the grill with oil before heating to prevent the jam from sticking.

PREP: 15 MINUTES   GRILL: ABOUT 15 MINUTES   MAKES 4 SERVINGS

1 tablespoon curry powder
1 tablespoon brown sugar
1 tablespoon olive oil
1/2 teaspoon salt
1/4 teaspoon ground cinnamon
pinch coarsely ground black pepper
1 garlic clove, crushed with
  garlic press

4 pork loin chops, each 3/4 inch
  thick (about 5 ounces each)
4 large peaches, each cut in half
  and pitted
1/2 cup peach or apricot jam or
  preserves

1. Prepare outdoor grill for direct grilling over medium heat.
2. In cup, stir curry powder, brown sugar, oil, salt, cinnamon, pepper, and garlic until blended. Rub curry mixture on both sides of pork chops.
3. Brush cut side of peach halves and one side of chops with some jam. Place peaches, jam side down, and chops, jam side up, on hot grill rack over medium heat; grill 5 minutes. Turn chops and peaches over and brush grilled side of chops with some jam; grill 5 minutes longer.
4. Remove peaches from grill when browned; place on platter. Turn chops and brush with remaining jam; grill until chops are browned on the outside and still slightly pink on the inside, 2 to 3 minutes longer. Place chops on platter with peaches.

Each serving: About 500 calories, 21g protein, 49g carbohydrate, 26g total fat (9g saturated), 77mg cholesterol, 360mg sodium.

TIP: Fresh peach halves, brushed with jam and grilled, make a wonderful summer dessert.

Pork Steaks with Plum Glaze

Our 1973 edition of *The Good Housekeeping Cookbook* explained how to cut a pork tenderloin into four lean and juicy steaks—a family secret from Zoe Coulson, *GH* food editor from 1968 to 1975. We used the same technique here: Slice tenderloin lengthwise almost in half, pound, then cut into serving-size pieces. Thanks, Zoe!

PREP: 10 MINUTES   GRILL: ABOUT 6 MINUTES   MAKES 4 SERVINGS

1 pork tenderloin (about 1 pound),
  trimmed
1 teaspoon salt
1/4 teaspoon coarsely ground
  black pepper
1/2 cup plum jam or preserves
1 tablespoon brown sugar
1 tablespoon grated, peeled fresh
  ginger

1 tablespoon fresh lemon juice
1/2 teaspoon ground cinnamon
2 garlic cloves, crushed with
  garlic press
4 large plums (about 1 pound), each
  cut in half and pitted

1. Prepare outdoor grill for direct grilling over medium heat.

2. Cut pork tenderloin lengthwise, almost in half, being careful not to cut all the way through. Open and spread flat. Place tenderloin between two sheets of plastic wrap; with meat mallet or rolling pin, pound to about 1/4-inch thickness. Cut tenderloin into 4 pieces; sprinkle with the salt and the pepper.

3. In small bowl, mix plum jam, brown sugar, ginger, lemon juice, cinnamon, and garlic. Brush one side of each pork steak and cut side of each plum half with plum-jam glaze.

4. Place pork and plums, glaze side down, on hot grill rack, over medium heat and grill 3 minutes. Brush steaks and plums with remaining glaze; turn and grill until steaks are lightly browned on both sides and just lost their pink color throughout and plums are hot, about 3 minutes longer.

Each serving: About 325 calories, 24g protein, 44g carbohydrate, 7g total fat (2g saturated), 71mg cholesterol, 65mg sodium.

Pork Steaks with Plum Glaze

Charbroiled Pork Chops with Corn Salsa

Charbroiled Pork Chops with Corn Salsa

Nothing says summer better than grilled meat and sweet corn. After fifteen minutes in marinade, meaty chops are flame-cooked, then topped with a quick garden salsa. Jalapeños vary in their degree of heat, so taste a small piece before you use it. If you'd like your salsa hotter, add more ground red pepper.

PREP: 15 MINUTES PLUS MARINATING   GRILL: 10 TO 12 MINUTES
MAKES 4 SERVINGS

2 tablespoons vegetable oil
2 tablespoons fresh lime juice
1/2 teaspoon salt
1/4 teaspoon ground red pepper
   (cayenne)
4 bone-in pork loin or rib chops,
   each 3/4 inch thick (about 6
   ounces each)

2 cups corn kernels cut from cobs
   (3 to 4 ears)
2 medium ripe tomatoes, chopped
1 small red onion, finely chopped
1 jalapeño chile, seeded and minced

1. In medium bowl, with wire whisk or fork, mix oil, lime juice, salt, and ground red pepper. Spoon half of oil mixture into pie plate. Add pork chops to mixture in pie plate, turning to coat. Marinate pork 15 minutes at room temperature or 30 minutes in the refrigerator, turning chops occasionally.
2. Prepare outdoor grill for direct grilling over medium heat.
3. Meanwhile, stir corn kernels, tomato, red onion, and jalapeño into oil mixture in bowl. Let salsa stand at room temperature until ready to serve.
4. Place pork chops on hot grill rack over medium heat; discard marinade in pie plate. Grill chops, turning once, until browned on the outside and still slightly pink on the inside, 10 to 12 minutes. Serve pork chops with corn salsa.

Each serving: About 420 calories, 23g protein, 22g carbohydrate, 28g total fat (9g saturated), 78mg cholesterol, 240mg sodium.

Teriyaki Pork Chops

We love this teriyaki sauce made with soy sauce, fresh ginger, and brown sugar. To prepare a fresh pineapple, use a sharp knife and cut off the leaves at the base, then slice off the bottom rind. Stand fruit upright and slice the rind from the sides in downward strokes. Remove any "eyes" that are left with the tip of a sharp knife.

PREP: 15 MINUTES PLUS MARINATING   GRILL: ABOUT 20 MINUTES
MAKES 4 SERVINGS

2 green onions, sliced
1/3 cup reduced-sodium soy sauce
2 tablespoons grated, peeled
   fresh ginger
2 tablespoons plus 1/4 cup packed
   light brown sugar

4 pork loin chops, 3/4 inch thick
   (about 8 ounces each)
1 small pineapple

1. In 13" by 9" glass baking dish, with fork, mix sliced green onions, soy sauce, ginger, and 2 tablespoons brown sugar. Add pork chops, turning to coat. Let stand 20 minutes at room temperature to marinate.
2. Prepare outdoor grill for direct grilling over medium heat.
3. Meanwhile, cut off rind from pineapple, then cut pineapple crosswise into 1/2-inch-thick slices. Sprinkle pineapple slices with remaining 1/4 cup brown sugar.
4. Place pineapple slices on hot grill rack over medium heat and grill, turning slices occasionally, until browned on both sides, 15 to 20 minutes. After pineapple has grilled 10 minutes, add pork chops and grill until lightly browned on both sides and chops just lose their pink color throughout, about 10 minutes. Turn chops occasionally and brush with remaining teriyaki mixture halfway through cooking time. Serve pork chops with grilled pineapple slices.

Each serving: About 645 calories, 33g protein, 48g carbohydrate, 37g total fat (13g saturated), 124mg cholesterol, 1,040mg sodium.

Cuban Mojo Pork Chops

Mojo (pronounced MO-ho) comes from the Spanish verb *mojar*, to wet. The seasoning mix is an integral component of Latin cuisine, used either as a condiment or as a base for a marinade. It traditionally was made with citrus juice, garlic, salt, and lard (now vegetable oil), but ingredients such as spices, herbs, onions, chiles, and even fruit make it extremely versatile.

PREP: 15 MINUTES PLUS MARINATING   GRILL: ABOUT 12 MINUTES
MAKES 4 SERVINGS

2 medium oranges
1/4 cup chopped onion
1/4 cup red wine vinegar
1 chipotle chile in adobo plus
   1 tablespoon adobo

4 garlic cloves
2 tablespoons fresh lime juice
1/4 teaspoon salt
4 bone-in pork loin chops, 3/4 inch
   thick (about 8 ounces each)

1. From oranges, grate 1/2 teaspoon peel and squeeze 1/2 cup juice.

2. In blender or food processor with knife blade attached, puree orange peel, onion, vinegar, chile, adobo, and garlic until smooth.

3. Pour marinade into large ziptight plastic bag; stir in orange and lime juices and salt. Add pork chops to marinade, turning to coat. Seal bag, pressing out excess air. Place bag on plate; let stand 15 minutes at room temperature or 1 hour in the refrigerator, turning several times.

4. Prepare outdoor grill for covered direct grilling over medium heat.

5. Remove chops from bag; pour marinade into 1-quart saucepan and reserve. Place chops on hot grill rack over medium heat. Cover grill and cook chops, turning once, until browned outside and still slightly pink in the center, 12 to 15 minutes.

6. Meanwhile, heat reserved marinade to boiling over high heat; boil 2 minutes.

7. Serve pork chops drizzled with cooked marinade.

Each serving: About 395 calories, 42g protein, 10g carbohydrate, 19g total fat (7g saturated), 116mg cholesterol, 410mg sodium.

Fennel-Orange Pork with Grilled Vegetables

Crushing the fennel seeds releases their flavor. The combination of fennel, thyme, and orange peel marries well with the richness of the pork. Radicchio and Belgian endive, with their slightly bitter taste, also serve as a counterbalance for the pork.

PREP: 15 MINUTES   GRILL: ABOUT 10 MINUTES   MAKES 4 SERVINGS

1 teaspoon fennel seeds
1/2 teaspoon dried thyme
1/4 teaspoon coarsely ground black pepper
3/4 teaspoon salt
1 teaspoon freshly grated orange peel
4 pork rib or loin chops, 1 inch thick (about 6 ounces each)
1 tablespoon olive oil

1 tablespoon balsamic vinegar
2 heads radicchio di Treviso (about 4 ounces each), each cut lengthwise in half, or 1 large round head radicchio (about 8 ounces), cut into 8 wedges
2 large heads Belgian endive (about 5 ounces each), each cut lengthwise into quarters

1. Prepare outdoor grill for direct grilling over medium heat.

2. In mortar with pestle or in ziptight plastic bag with rolling pin, crush fennel seeds with thyme, pepper, and $1/2$ teaspoon salt. Stir orange peel into fennel-seed mixture.

3. With hand, rub both sides of pork chops with fennel-seed mixture.

4. In medium bowl, mix oil, vinegar, and remaining $1/4$ teaspoon salt. Add radicchio and endive to bowl and gently toss to coat.

5. Place pork chops on grill over medium heat. Grill chops 5 minutes. Turn chops and add vegetables to grill. Grill pork chops and vegetables until chops have just a hint of pink color in center and vegetables are browned, about 5 minutes longer. Serve pork chops with grilled vegetables.

Each serving: About 250 calories, 23g protein, 5g carbohydrate, 15g total fat (4g saturated), 61mg cholesterol, 490mg sodium.

TIP: If you can't find radicchio, a burgundy-colored, slightly bitter Italian chicory, substitute 2 more heads of Belgian endive.

Fennel-Orange Pork
with Grilled Vegetables

Mixed Grill with Asian Flavors

Serve up a big platter of shrimp, pork, beef, and chicken flavored two ways—half with an herb rub and half with a teriyaki-style marinade—so guests can customize their main courses.

PREP: 1 HOUR PLUS MARINATING   GRILL: ABOUT 40 MINUTES
MAKES 20 SERVINGS

Soy Marinade (page 234)
Lime-Herb Rub (page 214)
2 beef flank steaks (1 1/4 pounds each)
2 whole pork tenderloins (1 pound each)
10 medium skinless, boneless chicken breast halves (6 ounces each)

40 large shrimp, shelled and deveined
Creamy Peanut Dipping Sauce (page 232)
8 (12-inch) metal skewers

1. In two separate, jumbo ziptight plastic bags, prepare Soy Marinade and Lime-Herb Rub. Add 1 flank steak, 1 pork tenderloin, and 5 chicken breast halves to each bag, turning to coat. Seal bags, pressing out excess air. Refrigerate 30 minutes or up to 1 hour. Add 20 shrimp to each bag during last 10 minutes of marinating time.
2. Prepare outdoor grill for direct grilling over medium heat.
3. Meanwhile, prepare Creamy Peanut Dipping Sauce.
4. Remove meat from bag with marinade; discard marinade. Remove meat from bag with rub. Thread 5 shrimp onto each skewer.
5. Place flank steaks and tenderloins on grill over medium heat. Grill flank steaks, turning once, 15 to 20 minutes for medium-rare or until desired doneness. Grill tenderloins, turning occasionally, until browned on the outside and slightly pink in the center, 20 minutes. Grill chicken breast halves, turning once, until juices run clear when thickest part is pierced with tip of knife, 10 to 12 minutes. Grill shrimp, turning skewers once, until opaque throughout, 4 to 6 minutes.
6. Thinly slice cooked meats; transfer to large platter. Cut chicken breast halves lengthwise in half; transfer chicken and shrimp to another platter. Serve with Creamy Peanut Dipping Sauce.

Each serving: About 380 calories, 48g protein, 10g carbohydrate, 15g total fat (4g saturated), 131mg cholesterol, 875mg sodium.

Sausage & Pepper Grill

Grill Italian hard rolls and serve the sausage and peppers on top for a hearty open-faced sandwich reminiscent of those found at street fairs. If you'd prefer, toss the grilled sausages and vegetables with a bowl of cooked ziti, add some grated Parmesan cheese, and serve.

PREP: 15 MINUTES   GRILL: 15 TO 20 MINUTES   MAKES 4 SERVINGS

1/3 cup balsamic vinegar
1 teaspoon brown sugar
1/2 teaspoon salt
1/4 teaspoon coarsely ground black pepper
2 medium red peppers, cut into 1 1/2-inch-wide strips
2 medium green peppers, cut into 1 1/2-inch-wide strips

2 large red onions (about 8 ounces each), each cut into 6 wedges
1 tablespoon olive oil
3/4 pound sweet Italian sausage links
3/4 pound hot Italian sausage links

1. Prepare outdoor grill for direct grilling over medium heat.

2. In cup, with fork, mix vinegar, brown sugar, salt, and black pepper. In large bowl, toss red and green peppers and onions with oil to coat.

3. Place sausages and vegetables on hot grill rack over medium heat and grill, turning occasionally, until golden brown and cooked through, 15 to 20 minutes. Cook vegetables, turning occasionally and brushing with some balsamic mixture during last 3 minutes of cooking, until tender, about 15 minutes. Transfer vegetables and sausages to platter as they finish cooking.

4. To serve, cut sausages diagonally into 2-inch slices. Drizzle remaining balsamic mixture over vegetables.

Each serving: About 500 calories, 27g protein, 19g carbohydrate, 36g total fat (12g saturated), 97mg cholesterol, 1,450mg sodium.

TIP: Adding a small amount of brown sugar to ordinary balsamic vinegar gives it a smooth, mellow flavor similar to that of an aged vinegar. Try this trick the next time you make a balsamic vinegar dressing.

Backyard BLTs

Our piquant lemon-herb mayonnaise makes this classic sandwich even better than ever!

PREP: 15 MINUTES   GRILL: 5 MINUTES   MAKES 4 SERVINGS

1 lemon
1/3 cup light mayonnaise
1 tablespoon chopped fresh parsley
1/2 teaspoon chopped fresh thyme
1/8 teaspoon coarsely ground
   black pepper
3 ripe medium tomatoes (about
   1 pound), cut into 1/4-inch-thick
   slices

1/8 teaspoon salt
8 slices (each 1/2 inch thick)
   sourdough bread
8 ounces thinly sliced Canadian
   bacon (about 24 slices)
8 small romaine lettuce leaves

1. Prepare outdoor grill for direct grilling over medium heat.

2. From lemon, grate 1/4 teaspoon peel and squeeze 1 teaspoon juice. In small bowl, mix lemon peel and lemon juice with mayonnaise, parsley, thyme, and pepper until blended; set aside. Place tomato slices on sheet of waxed paper and sprinkle with salt.

3. With tongs, place bread slices on hot grill rack over medium heat and grill just until grill marks appear on bottom side of bread. Remove bread slices from grill; set aside.

4. With tongs, place bacon slices on grill over medium heat and grill, just until grill marks appear on bacon, about 2 minutes (do not overcook; bacon will dry out and toughen).

5. To assemble sandwiches, spread mayonnaise mixture on ungrilled side of bread slices. Top half of bread slices with half of bacon slices, all of tomato slices, remaining bacon slices, then lettuce leaves. Place remaining bread slices, grilled side up, on top. Cut each sandwich in half to serve.

Each serving: About 315 calories, 17g protein, 32g carbohydrate, 14g total fat (2g saturated), 35mg cholesterol, 1,195mg sodium.

Backyard BLTs

Chile-Rubbed Ham with Peach Salsa

It's a quick grill—a fully cooked ham steak patted with paprika and smoky chiles before searing. Our soothing salsa tames the spice.

PREP: 30 MINUTES   GRILL: 4 TO 6 MINUTES   MAKES 4 SERVINGS

PEACH SALSA

4 ripe peaches (about 1 1/4 pounds), pitted and cut into 1/4-inch chunks
1 cup loosely packed fresh cilantro leaves, chopped
1 jalapeño chile, seeded and minced
2 tablespoons peach jam
2 tablespoons fresh lime juice
1/4 teaspoon salt

CHILE-RUBBED HAM

1 tablespoon paprika
1 tablespoon olive oil
2 teaspoons minced canned chipotle chile in adobo or 2 teaspoons adobo sauce
1 fully cooked center-cut ham steak, 1/2 inch thick (about 1 1/4 pounds)

1. Prepare outdoor grill for direct grilling over medium heat.

2. Prepare salsa: In medium bowl, toss peaches, cilantro, jalapeño, jam, lime juice, and salt. Cover and refrigerate salsa up to 1 day if not serving right away. Makes about 4 cups.

3. Prepare ham: In cup, mix paprika, oil, and chipotle chile. Spread mixture on both sides of ham.

4. Place ham on hot grill rack over medium-high heat; grill, turning ham once, until lightly browned and heated through, 4 to 6 minutes. Serve ham with salsa.

Each serving ham: About 180 calories, 24g protein, 1g carbohydrate, 8g total fat (2g saturated), 72mg cholesterol, 1,820mg sodium.

Each 1/2 cup salsa: About 40 calories, 0g protein, 10g carbohydrate, 0g total fat (0g saturated), 0mg cholesterol, 80mg sodium.

TIP: Canned chipotle chiles are smoked jalapeño chiles packed in a thick vinegary sauce called adobo. Look for chipotle chiles in Hispanic markets and in some supermarkets.

Butterflied Lamb with Moroccan Flavors

Fabulous exotic flavors with very little work! Serve with a cool, refreshing cucumber salad.

PREP: 15 MINUTES PLUS MARINATING   GRILL: 15 TO 25 MINUTES
MAKES 12 SERVINGS

1/3 cup loosely packed fresh cilantro
    leaves, chopped
1/4 cup olive oil
2 tablespoons dried mint, crumbled
2 teaspoons ground coriander
1 teaspoon ground ginger

1 teaspoon salt
1/2 teaspoon coarsely ground
    black pepper
1/2 teaspoon chili powder
3 1/2 pounds boneless butterflied
    lamb leg, trimmed

1. In small bowl, stir cilantro, oil, mint, coriander, ginger, salt, pepper, and chili powder.
2. Place lamb in 13" by 9" glass baking dish. Rub cilantro mixture on lamb to coat completely. Cover and refrigerate at least 1 hour or up to 4 hours.
3. Prepare outdoor grill for covered direct grilling over medium-low heat.
4. Place lamb on hot grill rack over medium-low heat. Cover grill and cook lamb, turning occasionally, 15 to 25 minutes for medium-rare or until desired doneness. Thickness of butterflied lamb will vary throughout; cut off sections of lamb as they are cooked and place on cutting board.
5. Let lamb stand 10 minutes to allow juices to set for easier slicing. Thinly slice lamb to serve.

Each serving: About 225 calories, 28g protein, 1g carbohydrate, 12g total fat (3g saturated), 88mg cholesterol, 270mg sodium.

TIP: Ask butcher to debone a 4 1/2-pound lamb leg shank half and slit the meat lengthwise to spread open like a thick steak.

Spiced Butterflied Lamb

For a cool and tangy sauce, a jar of mango chutney, available at the super-market, can be chopped and added to yogurt and served with the lamb. A crisp green or cucumber salad tossed with chopped fresh cilantro and basmati rice would be welcome additions to this Indian-style lamb.

PREP: 10 MINUTES PLUS MARINATING   GRILL: 25 TO 35 MINUTES
MAKES 10 SERVINGS

1 cup plain low-fat yogurt	2 tablespoons fresh lemon juice
8 garlic cloves, peeled	2 teaspoons salt
1 piece fresh ginger (about 2 inches), peeled and coarsely chopped	1/4 to 1/2 teaspoon ground red pepper (cayenne)
1 tablespoon ground coriander	3 pounds boneless butterflied
1 tablespoon ground cumin	leg of lamb (see Tip page 145)

1. In blender, puree yogurt, garlic, ginger, coriander, cumin, lemon juice, salt, and ground red pepper until smooth. Pour yogurt mixture into large ziptight plastic bag; add lamb, turning to coat. Seal bag, pressing out excess air. Place bag on plate; refrigerate lamb 1 hour, turning occasionally. (Do not marinate more than 2 hours or texture of meat will change.)

2. Prepare outdoor grill for direct grilling over medium heat.

3. Remove lamb from bag. Pour marinade into small bowl and reserve.

4. Place lamb on hot grill rack over medium heat and grill, turning once, 15 minutes. Brush both sides of lamb with reserved marinade and cook, turning lamb occasionally, 10 to 20 minutes longer for medium-rare or until desired doneness. Thickness of butterflied lamb will vary through-out; cut off sections of lamb as they are cooked and place on cutting board.

5. Let lamb stand 10 minutes to allow juices to set for easier slicing. Thinly slice lamb to serve.

Each serving: About 280 calories, 27g protein, 3g carbohydrate, 17g total fat (7g saturated), 95mg cholesterol, 550mg sodium.

TIP: For seedless juice, place a lemon half, cut side down, on a square of cheesecloth. Bring cheesecloth up over the top and tie with a twist-tie, then squeeze out the juice, seed free.

Spiced Butterflied Lamb

Miso-Glazed Salmon with Edamame Salad

SEAFOOD

Mediterranean Grilled Sea Bass

Grilled whole fish is a summer favorite in the Mediterranean. Sea bass is lovely on the grill; its firm white flesh holds up very well. If you can't get sea bass, substitute red snapper or striped bass.

PREP: 10 MINUTES PLUS MARINATING   GRILL: 12 TO 14 MINUTES
MAKES 4 SERVINGS

2 lemons
3 tablespoons olive oil
1 tablespoon chopped fresh oregano
   leaves
1 teaspoon ground coriander

1 1/4 teaspoons salt
2 whole sea bass, cleaned and scaled
   (about 1 1/2 pounds each)
1/4 teaspoon ground black pepper
2 large oregano sprigs

1. Prepare outdoor grill for covered direct grilling over medium heat.

2. Meanwhile, from 1 lemon, grate 1 tablespoon peel and squeeze 2 tablespoons juice. Cut one half of remaining lemon into slices; cut the remaining half into wedges. In small bowl, stir lemon juice and peel, oil, chopped oregano, coriander, and 1/4 teaspoon salt.

3. Rinse fish and pat dry with paper towels. Make 3 diagonal slashes in both sides of each fish. Sprinkle inside and out with pepper and remaining 1 teaspoon salt. Place lemon slices and oregano sprigs inside fish cavities. Place fish in 13" by 9" glass baking dish. Rub half of oil mixture on outside of both fish; reserve remaining oil mixture. Let stand 15 minutes at room temperature.

4. Place fish on hot rack over medium heat. Cover grill and cook fish, turning once, until just opaque throughout, 12 to 14 minutes.

5. To serve, place fish on cutting board. Working with one fish at a time, with knife, cut along backbone from head to tail. Slide wide metal spatula or cake server under front section of top fillet and lift off from backbone; transfer to platter. Gently pull out backbone and rib bones from bottom fillet and discard. Transfer bottom fillet to platter. Repeat with second fish. Drizzle fillets with remaining oil mixture. Serve with lemon wedges.

Each serving: About 305 calories, 40g protein, 1g carbohydrate, 15g total fat (3g saturated), 90mg cholesterol, 730mg sodium.

Mediterranean Grilled Sea Bass

Grilled Halibut with Fresh Dill

If fresh halibut is not available, substitute swordfish or tuna steaks. White-wine Worcestershire sauce is somewhat more delicate in flavor than the original Worcestershire and is particularly good with seafood and poultry. If you can't find white-wine Worcestershire, use 2 tablespoons of original Worcestershire and add 2 tablespoons of water.

PREP: 5 MINUTES PLUS MARINATING   GRILL: 10 MINUTES
MAKES 4 SERVINGS

1/4 cup white-wine Worcestershire
    sauce
2 tablespoons fresh lemon juice
1 tablespoon olive oil
1 tablespoon minced fresh dill

1/4 teaspoon coarsely ground black
    pepper
2 halibut steaks, each 1 inch thick
    (about 12 ounces each)

1. In medium bowl, stir Worcestershire, lemon juice, olive oil, dill, and pepper. Place halibut in large ziptight plastic bag. Add Worcestershire mixture. Seal bag, pressing out excess air. Place bag on plate; refrigerate up to 2 hours, turning bag over once.

2. Prepare outdoor grill for direct grilling over low heat.

3. Place halibut on hot grill rack over low heat, reserving marinade. Grill halibut, turning occasionally and basting frequently with reserved marinade, until opaque throughout, about 10 minutes.

Each serving: About 195 calories, 29g protein, 3g carbohydrate, 7g total fat (1g saturated), 45mg cholesterol, 200mg sodium.

TIP: Stir up an extra batch of the Worcestershire mixture and serve as a sauce for the fish.

Sicilian-Style Swordfish with Pasta

Chunks of grilled fish are tossed with pasta in a light vinaigrette made with fresh mint and tomato. If you can't find fresh mint, substitute fresh basil or parsley.

PREP: 15 MINUTES PLUS STANDING   GRILL: 8 TO 10 MINUTES
MAKES 6 SERVINGS

3 ripe medium tomatoes (1 pound), cut into 1/2-inch chunks (about 2 1/2 cups)	salt
	1/2 teaspoon coarsely ground black pepper
1/4 cup chopped fresh mint	1 teaspoon grated orange peel
1 tablespoon red wine vinegar	1 swordfish steak, 1 inch thick (about 1 pound)
1 small garlic clove, minced	
3 tablespoons olive oil	1 pound penne or bow-tie pasta

1. In large bowl, combine tomatoes, mint, vinegar, garlic, 2 tablespoons oil, 1/2 teaspoon salt, and 1/4 teaspoon pepper. Cover and let stand at room temperature 30 minutes.

2. Prepare outdoor grill for direct grilling over medium heat.

3. In cup, combine orange peel, remaining 1 tablespoon olive oil, 1/4 teaspoon salt, and remaining 1/4 teaspoon pepper. Brush mixture on both sides of swordfish.

4. Place swordfish on hot grill rack over medium heat. Grill swordfish, turning once, until just opaque throughout, 8 to 10 minutes. Transfer to cutting board and cut into 1-inch pieces.

5. Meanwhile, cook pasta in *boiling salted water* as label directs. Drain.

6. Add swordfish and pasta to tomato mixture; toss to combine.

Each serving: About 440 calories, 24g protein, 61g carbohydrate, 11g total fat (2g saturated), 26mg cholesterol, 430mg sodium.

Salmon with Mustard-Dill Sauce

We brought the flavors of Swedish gravlax to the grill. Traditional gravlax is made by marinating raw salmon in a savory mixture of fresh dill, sugar, and salt, then serving it with a sweet mustard sauce.

PREP: 15 MINUTES   GRILL: 8 TO 9 MINUTES   MAKES 4 SERVINGS

GRILLED SALMON
2 tablespoons sugar
1 tablespoon chopped fresh dill
2 tablespoons white wine vinegar
3/4 teaspoon salt
1/4 teaspoon coarsely ground black
  pepper
4 salmon steaks, each 3/4 inch thick
  (about 6 ounces each)

MUSTARD-DILL SAUCE
3 tablespoons chopped fresh dill
3 tablespoons Dijon mustard
3 tablespoons light mayonnaise
2 teaspoons sugar
4 teaspoons white wine vinegar
1/4 teaspoon coarsely ground black
  pepper

1. Prepare outdoor grill for direct grilling over medium heat.
2. Prepare salmon: In medium bowl, mix sugar, dill, vinegar, salt, and pepper.
3. With tweezers, remove any bones from salmon steaks. Add salmon to bowl with sugar mixture, turning to coat. Let stand at room temperature 10 minutes.
4. Meanwhile, prepare sauce: In small bowl, mix dill, mustard, mayonnaise, sugar, vinegar, and pepper.
5. Place salmon on hot grill rack over medium heat. Grill, turning once, just until opaque throughout, 8 to 9 minutes. Serve with mustard sauce.

Each serving: About 270 calories, 30g protein, 13g carbohydrate, 11g total fat (1g saturated), 80mg cholesterol, 850mg sodium.

Salmon Teriyaki

For an easy accompaniment, throw some green onions on the grill alongside the salmon. Turn them often; they'll take just a few minutes to cook.

PREP: 10 MINUTES   GRILL: 8 MINUTES   MAKES 4 SERVINGS

6 tablespoons teriyaki sauce
1 tablespoon brown sugar
1 teaspoon Asian sesame oil
4 salmon steaks, each 3/4 inch thick
(about 6 ounces each)

1 green onion, thinly sliced on
diagonal

1. Prepare outdoor grill for covered direct grilling over medium heat.
2. Meanwhile, in 2-quart saucepan, heat teriyaki sauce, sugar, and sesame oil to boiling over medium-high heat. Boil until slightly thickened, about 3 minutes.
3. Place salmon on hot rack over medium heat. Cover grill and cook salmon, turning once and brushing frequently with teriyaki mixture, until just opaque throughout, about 8 minutes.
4. Transfer salmon steaks to platter; sprinkle with green onion.

Each serving: About 320 calories, 36g protein, 8g carbohydrate, 15g total fat (3g saturated), 110mg cholesterol, 1,120mg sodium.

Spiced Salmon Steaks

Juicy summer-ripe red and yellow tomatoes are a cool and easy go-along for this entrée. Dress the tomatoes with a fruity olive oil and a sprinkling of finely shredded basil. Try this preparation with thick bluefish fillets; the spice mixture is a delicious complement to the richness of the fish.

PREP: 10 MINUTES   GRILL: ABOUT 8 MINUTES   MAKES 4 SERVINGS

1 tablespoon chili powder
2 teaspoons light brown sugar
1 teaspoon ground cumin
1 teaspoon dried thyme
1 teaspoon salt

2 teaspoons olive oil
4 salmon steaks, each 3/4 inch thick
  (about 8 ounces each)
lemon wedges (optional)

1. Prepare outdoor grill for direct grilling over medium heat.

2. In cup, mix chili powder, brown sugar, cumin, thyme, salt, and oil.

3. With tweezers, remove any bones from salmon. With hands, rub spice mixture on both sides of salmon steaks.

4. Place salmon on hot grill rack over medium heat. Grill salmon, turning once, until just opaque throughout, about 8 minutes. Serve with lemon wedges, if you like.

Each serving: About 405 calories, 40g protein, 4g carbohydrate, 24g total fat (5g saturated), 118mg cholesterol, 720mg sodium.

TIP: This recipe doubles easily. Prepare a double batch, serve half, and refrigerate the remainder. Serve the salmon chilled or at room temperature the next day.

Spiced Salmon Steaks

Salmon with Tomato-Olive Relish

Lightly season thick salmon steaks with *herbes de Provence*, a store-bought mix of dried herbs—often a combination of lavender, basil, thyme, and sage—that originated in southern France.

PREP: 25 MINUTES   GRILL: 8 MINUTES   MAKES 4 SERVINGS

TOMATO-OLIVE RELISH
1 lemon
1/2 cup green olives, pitted and
    coarsely chopped
1 medium tomato, cut into 1/4-inch
    chunks
1 tablespoon minced red onion

PROVENÇAL SALMON
1 tablespoon fennel seeds, crushed
2 teaspoons herbes de Provence
1 teaspoon freshly grated orange
    peel
3/4 teaspoon salt
4 salmon steaks, each 3/4 inch thick
    (about 6 ounces each)

1. Prepare relish: From lemon, grate 1/2 teaspoon peel and squeeze 1 tablespoon juice. In medium bowl, toss lemon peel and juice with olives, tomato, and red onion. Cover and refrigerate relish up to 1 day if not serving right away. Makes about 1 1/4 cups.

2. Prepare outdoor grill for covered direct grilling over medium heat.

3. Prepare salmon: In cup, mix fennel seeds, herbes de Provence, orange peel, and salt. Rub herb mixture on both sides of salmon.

4. Place salmon on hot rack over medium heat. Grill salmon, turning once, until just opaque throughout, 8 to 10 minutes. Serve salmon with Tomato-Olive Relish.

Each serving salmon: About 270 calories, 29g protein, 1g carbohydrate, 16g total fat (3g saturated), 80mg cholesterol, 515mg sodium.

Each 1/4 cup relish: About 25 calories, 0g protein, 3g carbohydrate, 2g total fat (0g saturated), 0mg cholesterol, 330mg sodium.

Salmon Steaks with Nectarine Salad

Fresh thyme adds wonderful fresh taste to this lightly spicy rub. If your super-market doesn't carry it, substitute 1/2 teaspoon dried thyme, crumbled.

PREP: 20 MINUTES   GRILL: ABOUT 8 MINUTES   MAKES 4 SERVINGS

1 tablespoon brown sugar
2 teaspoons vegetable oil
1 teaspoon ground coriander
1 1/2 teaspoons fresh thyme leaves
1 1/4 teaspoons salt
1/4 teaspoon coarsely ground
  black pepper
4 salmon steaks, each 3/4 inch thick
  (about 6 ounces each)

3 ripe nectarines (about 1 pound),
  pitted, each cut into quarters and
  thinly sliced crosswise
2 Kirby cucumbers (about 4 ounces
  each), each cut lengthwise in half,
  then thinly sliced crosswise
1 green onion, thinly sliced
1 tablespoon fresh lemon juice

1. Prepare outdoor grill for covered direct grilling over medium heat.

2. Meanwhile, in cup, combine brown sugar, oil, coriander, 1 teaspoon thyme, 3/4 teaspoon salt, and 1/8 teaspoon pepper. Rub mixture on both sides of salmon steaks.

3. In medium bowl, stir nectarines, cucumbers, green onion, lemon juice, remaining 1/2 teaspoon thyme, remaining 1/2 teaspoon salt, and remaining 1/8 teaspoon pepper. Makes about 4 1/2 cups.

4. Place salmon on hot rack over medium heat. Cover grill and cook salmon, turning once, until just opaque throughout, about 8 minutes. Serve with Nectarine Salad.

Each serving: About 355 calories, 29g protein, 18g carbohydrate, 18g total fat (3g saturated), 80mg cholesterol, 800mg sodium.

Miso-Glazed Salmon with Edamame Salad

Miso-Glazed Salmon with Edamame Salad

Spread a mixture of miso, ginger, and cayenne pepper on a large salmon fillet. Enjoy with our healthy soybean salad for a Japanese-inspired meal.

PREP: 30 MINUTES   GRILL: 10 TO 12 MINUTES   MAKES 4 SERVINGS

EDAMAME SALAD
1 bag (16 ounces) frozen shelled
   edamame (green soybeans) or
   frozen baby lima beans
1/4 cup seasoned rice vinegar
1 tablespoon vegetable oil
1 teaspoon sugar
3/4 teaspoon salt
1/8 teaspoon ground black pepper
1 bunch radishes (8 ounces), each
   cut in half and thinly sliced
1 cup loosely packed fresh cilantro
   leaves, chopped

MISO-GLAZED SALMON
2 tablespoons red miso
1 green onion, minced
1 tablespoon grated, peeled fresh
   ginger
1 teaspoon brown sugar
1/8 teaspoon ground red pepper
   (cayenne)
1 salmon fillet (1 1/2 pounds),
   with skin

1. Prepare salad: Cook edamame as label directs; drain. Rinse edamame with cold running water to stop cooking and drain again.
2. In medium bowl, whisk vinegar, oil, sugar, salt, and pepper until blended. Add edamame, radishes, and cilantro and toss until evenly coated. Cover and refrigerate salad up to 1 day if not serving right away. Makes about 4 cups.
3. Prepare outdoor grill for direct grilling over medium–low heat.
4. Prepare salmon: In small bowl, with spoon, mix miso, green onion, ginger, brown sugar, and ground red pepper. Rub miso mixture on flesh side of salmon.
5. Place salmon, skin side down, on hot rack over medium–low heat. Grill salmon until just opaque throughout, 10 to 12 minutes. Serve with Edamame Salad.

Each serving salmon: About 280 calories, 29g protein, 3g carbohydrate, 16g total fat (3g saturated), 80mg cholesterol, 450mg sodium.

Each 1 cup salad: About 220 calories, 16g protein, 23g carbohydrate, 8g total fat (0g saturated), 0mg cholesterol, 1,020mg sodium.

Honey-Lime Salmon

Rich salmon fillets stand up to an assertively spiced rub. You can rub and refrigerate the salmon up to eight hours before grilling. On the side, serve coleslaw dressed with a vinaigrette or a salad of thickly sliced summer tomatoes and crunchy cucumbers.

PREP: 10 MINUTES   GRILL: 8 TO 9 MINUTES   MAKES 4 SERVINGS

3 tablespoons honey
1 teaspoon ground cumin
1 teaspoon ground coriander
3/4 teaspoon salt
3/4 teaspoon grated fresh lime peel
1/4 teaspoon coarsely ground black
  pepper

1 teaspoon very hot water
4 pieces salmon fillet, 3/4 inch
  thick (about 6 ounces each),
  skin removed
3 tablespoons chopped fresh cilantro
lime wedges

1. Prepare outdoor grill for direct grilling over medium heat.

2. In cup, mix honey, cumin, coriander, salt, lime peel, pepper, and water until blended.

3. With tweezers, remove any bones from salmon. With hands, rub honey-spice mixture on salmon pieces.

4. Place salmon on hot grill rack over medium heat. Grill salmon, turning once, just until salmon turns opaque throughout, 8 to 9 minutes.

5. Sprinkle salmon with cilantro and serve with lime wedges.

Each serving: About 350 calories, 32g protein, 14g carbohydrate, 18g total fat (4g saturated), 95mg cholesterol, 535mg sodium.

TIP: You can substitute red snapper or bluefish fillets for the salmon.

Pepper-Rubbed Salmon with Melon Salsa

You could use all white, green, black, or pink peppercorns if you don't have mixed pepper blend on hand. Fresh, coarsely ground peppercorns are much tastier than the store-bought ground pepper, so if you don't already own one, a pepper grinder is a wise investment.

PREP: 25 MINUTES   GRILL: ABOUT 14 MINUTES   MAKES 8 SERVINGS

Melon Salsa (page 224)
1 tablespoon mixed pepper blend
   (white, green, black, and pink
   whole peppercorns)
1 1/2 teaspoons ground coriander

1 1/2 teaspoons grated fresh lemon
   peel
3/4 teaspoon salt
1 center-cut salmon fillet with skin
   on (3 pounds)
cilantro sprigs for garnish

1. Prepare Melon Salsa.

2. Prepare outdoor grill for covered direct grilling over medium heat.

3. Meanwhile, prepare salmon: Coarsely grind pepper blend in pepper grinder. In small bowl, combine ground pepper, coriander, lemon peel, and salt. Pat pepper mixture onto flesh side of salmon. (For easier handling, cut salmon crosswise into two pieces.)

4. Place salmon, flesh side down, on hot grill rack over medium heat. Cook, just to sear and mark salmon, 2 to 3 minutes. Turn salmon over. Cover grill and cook salmon until just opaque throughout, 12 to 14 minutes longer.

5. Transfer salmon to platter. Serve with Melon Salsa.

Each serving: About 270 calories, 29g protein, 1g carbohydrate, 16g total fat (3g saturated), 82mg cholesterol, 300mg sodium.

Salmon with Dill and Caper Sauce

Anchovy paste is available in tubes in the dairy section of many supermarkets. If you can't find anchovy paste, substitute 2 anchovy fillets. Mash the fillets with the flat side of a knife until they're the consistency of a smooth paste. Serve the salmon with Cucumber Relish (page 235), if you like.

PREP: 10 MINUTES   GRILL: ABOUT 10 MINUTES   MAKES 8 SERVINGS

1/4 cup drained capers, chopped
2 tablespoons fresh dill, chopped
2 tablespoons fresh lemon juice
2 teaspoons sugar

2 teaspoons anchovy paste
1 salmon fillet (2 pounds), with skin
1/4 teaspoon salt
lemon wedges

1. Prepare outdoor grill for direct grilling over medium heat.

2. In small bowl, mix capers, dill, lemon juice, sugar, and anchovy paste.

3. With tweezers, remove any bones from salmon; sprinkle with salt. Place salmon in lightly oiled fish basket and brush all of caper sauce on flesh side only.

4. Place fish basket on hot grill rack over medium heat. Grill salmon, turning once, until just opaque throughout, about 10 minutes. Serve with lemon wedges.

Each serving: About 210 calories, 22g protein, 2g carbohydrate, 12g total fat (2g saturated), 64mg cholesterol, 395mg sodium.

TIP: Mix chopped dill or tarragon, fresh lemon juice, a fruity olive oil, salt, and pepper and serve as a sauce to spoon over any grilled fish.

Salmon with Dill and Caper Sauce

Glazed Salmon with Watermelon Salsa

We love the combination of sweet and spicy flavors so we added a jalapeño chile to the fruit salsa—with delicious results.

PREP: 20 MINUTES   GRILL: ABOUT 9 MINUTES   MAKES 4 SERVINGS

WATERMELON SALSA
1 lime
4 cups (1/2-inch cubes) seedless watermelon (from about 2 1/2-pound piece)
1/4 cup loosely packed fresh mint leaves, chopped
2 tablespoons chopped green onions
1 small jalapeño chile, seeded and finely chopped (1 tablespoon)

GLAZED SALMON
1/4 cup hoisin sauce
1/2 teaspoon Chinese five-spice powder
4 salmon steaks, 1 inch thick (about 6 ounces each)

1. Prepare outdoor grill for covered direct grilling over medium heat.

2. Meanwhile, prepare salsa: From lime, grate 1 teaspoon peel and squeeze 1 tablespoon juice. In serving bowl, toss lime peel and juice with watermelon, mint, green onions, and jalapeño. Makes about 3 2/3 cups.

3. Prepare salmon: In cup, stir hoisin sauce and five-spice powder.

4. Place salmon on hot grill rack over medium heat. Brush salmon with half of hoisin mixture. Cover grill and cook salmon 3 minutes. Turn salmon over and brush with remaining hoisin mixture. Cover grill and cook 3 minutes. Turn salmon over again and cook until just opaque throughout, about 3 more minutes. Serve salmon with Watermelon Salsa.

Each serving About 345 calories, 30g protein, 18g carbohydrate, 17g total fat (3g saturated), 81mg cholesterol, 260mg sodium.

Glazed Salmon with Watermelon Salsa

Jamaican Jerk Catfish with Grilled Pineapple

Jamaican Jerk Catfish with Grilled Pineapple

Other fish fillets like sole, flounder, snapper, and bluefish work well with these zesty flavors, too. A very versatile seasoning, jerk also does wonders for grilled chicken and pork. Add another jalapeño or some crushed red peppers if you'd like a spicier jerk.

PREP: 15 MINUTES   GRILL: 10 TO 12 MINUTES   MAKES 4 SERVINGS

2 green onions, chopped
1 jalapeño chile, seeded and chopped
2 tablespoons white wine vinegar
2 tablespoons Worcestershire sauce
1 tablespoon minced, peeled fresh ginger
1 tablespoon vegetable oil
1 1/4 teaspoons dried thyme

1 teaspoon ground allspice
1/4 teaspoon salt
4 catfish fillets (about 5 ounces each)
1 small pineapple, cut lengthwise into 4 wedges or crosswise into 1/2-inch-thick slices
2 tablespoons brown sugar

1. Prepare outdoor grill for direct grilling over medium-high heat.

2. In medium bowl, mix green onions, jalapeño, vinegar, Worcestershire, ginger, oil, thyme, allspice, and salt until combined. Add catfish fillets to bowl, turning to coat; let stand 5 minutes at room temperature.

3. Meanwhile, rub pineapple wedges or slices with brown sugar.

4. Place pineapple and catfish fillets on hot grill rack over medium-high heat. Brush half of jerk mixture remaining in bowl on catfish; grill 5 minutes. Turn pineapple and catfish. Brush remaining jerk mixture on fish and grill until fish is just opaque throughout and pineapple is golden brown, 5 to 7 minutes longer.

Each serving: About 350 calories, 23g protein, 35g carbohydrate, 14g total fat (3g saturated), 47mg cholesterol, 280mg sodium.

TIP: Fresh jalapeño peppers vary in their degree of heat, while pickled jalapeños from a jar are always hot. Feel free to substitute jarred for fresh in most recipes.

Thai Snapper

Tender fillets are seasoned with lime and ginger and cooked in a foil packet. Don't be tempted to assemble the packets too soon before grilling; the lime juice will start to "cook" the fillets, giving them a mushy texture. Instead, cut the vegetables and prepare the lime juice mixture several hours ahead and assemble the packets just before cooking.

PREP: 30 MINUTES   GRILL: 8 MINUTES   MAKES 4 SERVINGS

3 tablespoons fresh lime juice
1 tablespoon Asian fish sauce
1 tablespoon olive oil
1 teaspoon grated, peeled fresh
  ginger
1/2 teaspoon sugar
1/2 teaspoon minced garlic

4 (16" by 12") foil sheets
4 red snapper fillets (6 ounces each)
1 large carrot, peeled and cut into
  2 1/4-inch-long matchstick strips
1 large green onion, thinly sliced
1/4 cup packed fresh cilantro leaves

1. Prepare outdoor grill for direct grilling over medium heat.
2. In small bowl, mix lime juice, fish sauce, oil, ginger, sugar, and garlic.
3. Fold each foil sheet crosswise in half and open up again. Place 1 fillet, skin side down, on one half of each foil sheet. Top each with carrot, green onion, and cilantro. Spoon lime juice mixture over snapper and vegetables. Fold unfilled half of foil over fish. To seal packets, beginning at a corner where foil is folded, make small 1/2-inch folds, with each new fold overlapping previous one, until packet is completely sealed. Packet will resemble half-circle.
4. Place packets on hot grill rack over medium heat; cook 8 minutes.
5. To serve, with kitchen shears, cut an X in top of each packet to allow steam to escape.

Each serving: About 230 calories, 36g protein, 5g carbohydrate, 6g total fat (1g saturated), 63mg cholesterol, 270mg sodium.

TIP: Asian fish sauce (*nuoc nam* or *nam pla*) is a thin, translucent, salty, brown liquid extracted from salted, fermented fish. This condiment is used mostly in Thai and Vietnamese cooking. It can be purchased in the Asian sections of some grocery stores.

Asian Tuna Burgers

Finely chop fish by hand for a light texture; using a food processor will make the patties dense and dry. Serve with pickled ginger, with or without a bun. Cucumber Relish (page 235) would be the perfect condiment to serve with these tasty burgers.

PREP: 15 MINUTES   GRILL: 6 TO 7 MINUTES   MAKES 4 SERVINGS

1 tuna steak (about 1 pound)
1 green onion, thinly sliced
2 tablespoons reduced-sodium
  soy sauce
1 teaspoon grated, peeled fresh
  ginger

1/4 teaspoon coarsely ground black
  pepper
1/4 cup plain dried bread crumbs
2 tablespoons sesame seeds
Nonstick cooking spray

1. Prepare outdoor grill for direct grilling over medium heat.

2. With large chef's knife, finely chop tuna. Place tuna in medium bowl. Add green onion, soy sauce, ginger, and pepper; mix until combined (mixture will be very soft and moist). Shape tuna mixture into four 3-inch round patties.

3. On waxed paper, combine bread crumbs and sesame seeds. With hands, carefully press patties, one at a time, into bread-crumb mixture, turning to coat both sides. Spray both sides of tuna patties with nonstick spray.

4. Place patties on hot grill rack over medium heat and grill, turning once, until browned on the outside and still slightly pink in the center for medium-rare or until desired doneness, 6 to 7 minutes.

Each serving: About 210 calories, 26g protein, 7g carbohydrate, 8g total fat (2g saturated), 38mg cholesterol, 400mg sodium.

TIP: If you can't imagine a burger of any sort without ketchup, try a combination of Chinese hoisin sauce and ketchup as a topping.

Shrimp Sonoma

Some of the sweetest dried tomatoes we've tried come from the Sonoma Valley in California. Choose dried tomatoes that are plump rather than dry and leathery. Make a batch of Veggie Kabobs (page 207) and grill them alongside the shrimp. Serve on a bed of couscous seasoned with extravirgin olive oil.

PREP: 25 MINUTES   GRILL: 8 TO 10 MINUTES   MAKES 6 SERVINGS

1 ounce dried tomatoes without salt	2 tablespoons olive oil
1 cup boiling water	1/2 teaspoon salt
1 1/2 pounds large shrimp	1/2 teaspoon crushed red pepper
2 tablespoons fresh lemon juice	4 (12-inch) metal skewers

1. Place dried tomatoes in small bowl. Pour boiling water over tomatoes; let stand while preparing shrimp.

2. Meanwhile, pull off legs from shrimp. Insert tip of kitchen shears under shell of each shrimp and snip along back to tail, cutting about 1/4 inch deep to expose dark vein. Leaving shell on, rinse shrimp to remove vein; pat dry with paper towels. Place shrimp in bowl.

3. Prepare outdoor grill for direct grilling over medium heat.

4. Drain dried tomatoes, reserving 1/4 cup soaking liquid.

5. In blender or in food processor with knife blade attached, puree tomatoes, reserved soaking liquid, lemon juice, olive oil, salt, and crushed red pepper until smooth. Pour over shrimp.

6. Thread shrimp onto metal skewers. Place skewers on hot grill rack over medium heat. Grill shrimp, turning skewers occasionally and basting with any remaining dried tomato mixture, until just opaque throughout, 8 to 10 minutes.

Each serving: About 140 calories, 20g protein, 3g carbohydrate, 5g total fat (1g saturated), 140mg cholesterol, 290mg sodium.

TIP: When shopping for shrimp, look for firm, shiny shells without any black spots.

Shrimp Sonoma

Shrimp Saté with Cucumber Salad

An aromatic rice such as jasmine or basmati makes a delicious accompaniment to this Indonesian-inspired dish.

PREP: 45 MINUTES PLUS MARINATING   GRILL: 4 TO 5 MINUTES
MAKES 4 SERVINGS

8 (7-inch) bamboo skewers
1 tablespoon vegetable oil
6 tablespoons fresh lime juice (from 3 to 4 limes)
3 tablespoons minced cilantro
1/2 teaspoon salt
1/2 teaspoon crushed red pepper
1 pound large shrimp, shelled and deveined

2 small cucumbers (about 8 ounces each)
2 tablespoons sugar
1 tablespoon snipped fresh chives
2 tablespoons slivered fresh basil leaves
3 tablespoons chopped roasted salted peanuts

1. Prepare outdoor grill for direct grilling over medium heat.

2. Soak skewers in water to cover for 30 minutes. Drain before using.

3. While skewers soak, in medium bowl, whisk together oil, 3 tablespoons lime juice, 2 tablespoons cilantro, 1/4 teaspoon salt, and 1/4 teaspoon crushed red pepper. Stir in shrimp and marinate at room temperature 15 minutes.

4. Meanwhile, cut each unpeeled cucumber lengthwise in half. With spoon, scoop out seeds. Thinly slice cucumber halves crosswise. In another medium bowl, stir cucumbers, sugar, chives, 1 tablespoon basil, remaining 3 tablespoons lime juice, 1 tablespoon cilantro, 1/4 teaspoon salt, and 1/4 teaspoon crushed red pepper. Set aside. Makes about 3 cups.

5. Thread about 4 shrimp on each skewer. With long-handled basting brush, lightly oil grill rack. Place skewers on hot rack. Cook shrimp just until opaque throughout, turning over once, 4 to 5 minutes.

6. Spoon cucumber salad onto 4 dinner plates; sprinkle with peanuts. Arrange skewers with shrimp over salad. Sprinkle with remaining basil.

Each serving: About 205 calories, 22g protein, 13g carbohydrate, 8g total fat (1g saturated), 180mg cholesterol, 555mg sodium.

Grilled Shrimp with Black Beans

Tex-Mex black bean salad turns into a great summer supper when you add grilled shrimp. Rinsing the black beans removes excess sodium.

PREP: 15 MINUTES   GRILL: 3 TO 4 MINUTES   MAKES 4 SERVINGS

1 lime
2 cans (15 to 19 ounces each) black
  beans, rinsed and drained
2 ripe plum tomatoes (about
  8 ounces), chopped
2 green onions, thinly sliced
1 small yellow pepper, seeded and
  chopped

1 jalapeño chile, seeded and finely
  chopped
1/2 cup loosely packed fresh cilantro
  leaves, chopped
1 tablespoon olive oil
3/4 teaspoon salt
1 pound large shrimp, peeled and
  deveined
lime wedges

1. Prepare outdoor grill for direct grilling over medium-high heat.

2. Meanwhile, from lime, grate 1/2 teaspoon peel and squeeze 2 tablespoons juice. In large bowl, stir lime juice, 1/4 teaspoon peel, beans, tomatoes, green onions, yellow pepper, jalapeño, cilantro, oil, and 1/2 teaspoon salt. Set aside at room temperature while you grill shrimp. Makes about 5 cups.

3. Rinse shrimp with cold running water; pat dry with paper towels. In medium bowl, toss shrimp with remaining 1/4 teaspoon lime peel and 1/4 teaspoon salt.

4. Place shrimp on hot grill rack (or hot flat grill topper) over medium-high heat and grill shrimp, turning once, just until opaque throughout, 3 to 4 minutes.

5. Stir about half of shrimp into bean salad; top with remaining shrimp. Serve with lime wedges.

Each serving: About 290 calories, 31g protein, 41g carbohydrate, 5g total fat (1g saturated), 180mg cholesterol, 890mg sodium.

Shrimp and Scallop Kabobs

Shrimp and scallops cook in a flash and require no marinating. If the scallops are very large, halve them horizontally. Don't substitute bay scallops; they're small and will cook too quickly. If you like, serve with Pineapple Salsa (page 223) and a bowl of rice.

PREP: 20 MINUTES   GRILL: 6 TO 8 MINUTES   MAKES 6 SERVINGS

1 pound large shrimp
1 pound large sea scallops
3 tablespoons soy sauce
3 tablespoons seasoned rice vinegar
2 tablespoons grated, peeled fresh ginger
1 tablespoon brown sugar

1 tablespoon Asian sesame oil
2 garlic cloves, crushed with garlic press
1 bunch green onions, cut diagonally into 3-inch-long pieces
12 cherry tomatoes
6 (12-inch) metal skewers

1. Prepare outdoor grill for direct grilling over medium heat.
2. Shell and devein shrimp, leaving tail part of shell on, if you like; rinse with cold running water. Rinse scallops. Pat shrimp and scallops dry with paper towels.
3. In large bowl, mix soy sauce, rice vinegar, ginger, brown sugar, sesame oil, and garlic. Add shrimp and scallops; toss until evenly coated.
4. Alternately thread shrimp, scallops, green onions, and cherry tomatoes onto metal skewers. Place skewers on hot grill rack over medium heat; grill shrimp and scallops, turning skewers occasionally, and basting with any remaining soy-sauce mixture halfway through cooking, until just opaque throughout, 6 to 8 minutes.

Each serving: About 185 calories, 26g protein, 10g carbohydrate, 4g total fat (1g saturated), 118mg cholesterol, 880mg sodium.

TIP: The soy mixture can be made several hours in advance, covered, and refrigerated. Whisk to combine before adding the shrimp and scallops.

Shrimp and Scallop Kabobs

Cajun Shrimp with Rémoulade Sauce

This takes only four minutes on the fire! We added fresh lemon peel to jarred Cajun seasoning (a blend of garlic, onion, chiles, peppers, and herbs). Seasoning mixes vary among manufacturers, especially with regard to salt content. Add salt to taste if necessary.

PREP: 25 MINUTES   GRILL: 3 TO 4 MINUTES   MAKES 4 SERVINGS

RÉMOULADE SAUCE
- 1/2 cup light mayonnaise
- 2 tablespoons ketchup
- 2 tablespoons minced celery
- 1 tablespoon Dijon mustard with seeds
- 1 tablespoon minced fresh parsley
- 2 teaspoons fresh lemon juice
- 1/2 teaspoon Cajun seasoning
- 1 green onion, minced

CAJUN SHRIMP
- 1 tablespoon Cajun seasoning
- 1 tablespoon olive oil
- 2 teaspoons fresh lemon peel
- 1 1/4 pounds large shrimp, shelled and deveined, leaving tail part of shell on, if you like
- lemon wedges

1. Prepare outdoor grill for direct grilling over medium-high heat.

2. Prepare sauce: In small bowl, mix mayonnaise, ketchup, celery, mustard, parsley, lemon juice, Cajun seasoning, and green onion. Cover and refrigerate up to 3 days if not serving right away. Makes about 1 cup.

3. Prepare shrimp: In medium bowl, mix Cajun seasoning, oil, and lemon peel. Add shrimp to spice mixture and toss until evenly coated.

4. Place shrimp on hot grill rack (or hot flat grill topper) over medium-high heat and grill, turning once, just until opaque throughout, 3 to 4 minutes.

5. Transfer shrimp to platter; serve with Rémoulade Sauce and the lemon wedges.

Each serving shrimp: About 155 calories, 24g protein, 2g carbohydrate, 5g total fat (1g saturated), 175mg cholesterol, 575mg sodium.

Each 1 tablespoon sauce: About 30 calories, 0g protein, 2g carbohydrate, 3g total fat (1g saturated), 3mg cholesterol, 95mg sodium.

Garlicky Grilled Clams and Mussels

Buy your shellfish from a reputable purveyor and plan to serve them the same day of purchase. If you're not cooking right away, store them in a large bowl covered with a wet towel in the refrigerator, not on ice, until the grill is ready.

PREP: 20 MINUTES   GRILL: ABOUT 10 MINUTES
MAKES 8 FIRST-COURSE OR 4 MAIN-DISH SERVINGS

4 tablespoons butter or margarine,
  cut into pieces
2 tablespoons olive oil
3 garlic cloves, minced
1 large shallot, minced ($1/4$ cup)
$1/2$ cup dry white wine
$1/4$ teaspoon crushed red pepper

2 pounds mussels, scrubbed, with
  beards removed
2 dozen littleneck clams, scrubbed
$2/3$ cup loosely packed fresh parsley
  leaves, coarsely chopped
lemon and/or lime wedges
French bread slices

1. Prepare outdoor grill for covered direct grilling over medium-high heat.
2. Place butter and oil in large disposable foil roasting pan (about 16" by 12 1/2"). Place pan on hot grill rack over medium-high heat and heat until butter has melted. Remove pan from grill. Add garlic, shallot, wine, and crushed red pepper; stir to combine. Add mussels and clams, spreading out to an even layer. Cover pan tightly with foil.
3. Return pan to grill rack. Cover grill and cook until mussels and clams open, 8 to 10 minutes.
4. Discard any mussels or clams that have not opened. Sprinkle with parsley and serve with lemon and/or lime wedges and French bread.

Each serving: About 360 calories, 28g protein, 10g carbohydrate, 22g total fat (14g saturated), 130mg cholesterol, 408mg sodium.

VEGETABLES & SIDE DISHES

Grilled Eggplant, Peppers,
Zucchini, and Summer Squash

Chiles Relleños

If you prefer hotter flavor, after grilling and before filling the chiles, remove the seeds and veins but don't rinse the insides. Serve the chiles with salsa, if you like, but be aware that poblanos can sometimes be very hot; so choose your salsa accordingly. If you have access to a Latin American market, look for *queso blanco* and use it in place of the Monterey Jack.

PREP: 20 MINUTES   GRILL: 20 TO 25 MINUTES
MAKES 6 ACCOMPANIMENT SERVINGS

6 medium poblano chiles (about 4
    ounces each)
6 ounces Monterey Jack cheese,
    shredded (1 1/2 cups)

1 cup corn kernels cut from cobs
    (about 2 medium ears)
1/2 cup loosely packed fresh cilantro
    leaves, chopped

1. Prepare outdoor grill for direct grilling over medium heat.
2. Place whole chiles on hot grill rack over medium heat and cook, turning occasionally, until blistered and blackened on all sides, 10 to 15 minutes.
3. Transfer chiles to large sheet of foil. Wrap chiles in foil, seal tightly, and allow to steam at room temperature until cool enough to handle, about 15 minutes.
4. Meanwhile, in medium bowl, combine cheese, corn, and cilantro.
5. Remove chiles from foil. Cut 2-inch lengthwise slit in side of each chile, being careful not to cut through top or bottom. Under cold running water, gently peel off skin. Remove seeds and veins from opening; rinse with running water. Pat chiles dry with paper towels.
6. With spoon, fill each chile with about 1/2 cup cheese mixture. Gently reshape chiles to close opening. Place 3 filled chiles in single layer on each of two 18" by 18" sheets of heavy-duty foil. Bring two sides of foil up and fold several times to seal. Fold over ends to seal in juices. (Chiles can be prepared to this point and refrigerated up to 6 hours before grilling.)
7. Place foil packet on hot grill rack over medium heat and cook until chiles are heated through and cheese has melted, about 10 minutes.

Each serving: About 160 calories, 9g protein, 13g carbohydrate, 9g total fat (5g saturated), 30mg cholesterol, 160mg sodium.

Hot Buttered Chili-Lime Corn

Serve sweet corn hot off the grill already buttered and seasoned.

PREP: 15 MINUTES   GRILL: 12 MINUTES
MAKES 4 ACCOMPANIMENT SERVINGS

4 ears corn, husks and silk removed, and each ear cut crosswise in half
2 tablespoons butter or margarine, softened
1 teaspoon chili powder
1/2 teaspoon salt
1/2 teaspoon fresh lime peel
fresh lime wedges (optional)

1. Prepare outdoor grill for direct grilling over medium heat.

2. Place corn in 14 1/2" by 12 1/2" extra-heavy-duty foil cooking bag in single layer. In cup, stir butter, chili powder, salt, and lime peel until blended. Dot mixture on corn and fold bag to seal as label directs.

3. Place foil packet on hot grill rack over medium heat. Cook corn, turning packet over once halfway through cooking, 12 minutes. Remove packet from grill.

4. Before serving, with kitchen shears, cut an X in top of foil packet to let steam escape, then carefully pull back foil to open. Serve corn with lime wedges, if you like.

Each serving: About 115 calories, 3g protein, 17g carbohydrate, 5g total fat (4g saturated), 31mg cholesterol, 242mg sodium.

TIP: Look for foil cooking bags in your supermarket where foil and plastic wrap are sold. If you can't find them, you can make your own: Layer two 20" by 18" sheets heavy-duty foil to make a double thickness. Place recipe ingredients on center of foil. Bring short ends of foil up and over ingredients and fold over two to three times to seal well. Fold over remaining sides of foil two or three times to seal in juices.

Corn on the Cob with Molasses Butter

Cayenne pepper and coriander add kick to this molasses-sweetened butter.

PREP: 10 MINUTES   GRILL: 10 TO 15 MINUTES
MAKES 8 ACCOMPANIMENT SERVINGS

2 tablespoon butter or margarine,
  softened
1 teaspoon light (mild) molasses
1/2 teaspoon ground coriander

1/2 teaspoon salt
pinch ground red pepper (cayenne)
8 ears corn, husks and silk removed

1. Prepare outdoor grill for covered direct grilling over medium-high heat.
2. In small bowl, with fork, stir butter, molasses, coriander, salt, and ground red pepper until well combined.
3. Place corn on hot grill rack over medium-high heat. Cover grill and cook corn, turning frequently, until brown in spots, 10 to 15 minutes.
4. Transfer corn to platter; spread each ear with molasses butter.

Each serving: About 105 calories, 3g protein, 18g carbohydrate, 4g total fat (2g saturated), 8mg cholesterol, 186mg sodium.

Campfire Corn with Herb Butter

Campfire Corn with Herb Butter

Roasting brings out the nutty flavor of fresh corn on the cob, and leaving the husks on prevents the delicate kernels from drying out. For an added taste treat, serve the corn with wedges of lemon or lime; the tart citrus flavor complements the sweetness of the corn.

PREP: 15 MINUTES PLUS SOAKING   GRILL: 20 TO 30 MINUTES
MAKES 6 ACCOMPANIMENT SERVINGS

6 medium ears corn, with husks and silk	2 tablespoons minced fresh parsley
6 (8-inch) pieces kitchen twine	1 teaspoon minced fresh tarragon
1 medium shallot, minced	1 teaspoon freshly grated lemon peel
3 tablespoons butter or margarine, softened	1/2 teaspoon salt
	1 1/8 teaspoons ground black pepper

1. Prepare outdoor grill for direct grilling over medium heat.
2. Gently pull husks three-fourths of way down on each ear of corn; remove silk. In large saucepot or kettle, place corn with husks and kitchen twine. Add enough *water to cover*; let soak for at least 15 minutes. (Soaking corn with husks in water helps keep husks from burning on grill.)
3. Meanwhile, in small bowl, stir shallot, butter, parsley, tarragon, lemon peel, salt, and pepper. Let stand at room temperature up to 20 minutes or refrigerate overnight, if you like.
4. Remove corn from water; drain well. With pastry brush, brush each ear with some butter mixture. Pull husks back up and, with twine, tie them at top of ears.
5. Place corn on hot grill rack over medium heat. Grill, turning occasionally, until husks are brown and dry and kernels are tender, 20 to 30 minutes.

Each serving: About 140 calories, 3g protein, 20g carbohydrate, 7g total fat (4g saturated), 16mg cholesterol, 252mg sodium.

TIP: Can't find shallots? Substitute finely chopped red or green onion.

Corn and Jack Quesadillas

We added a romaine salad to make a complete meal. To save time, slice the lettuce for the salad and grate the cheese for the quesadillas while the corn is grilling.

PREP: 10 MINUTES PLUS COOLING   GRILL: 11 TO 17 MINUTES
MAKES 4 SERVINGS

3 large ears corn, husks and silk removed

4 low-fat burrito-size (8- to 10-inch diameter) flour tortillas

4 ounces reduced-fat Monterey Jack cheese, shredded (1 cup)

1/2 cup mild or medium-hot salsa

2 green onions, thinly sliced

1 head romaine lettuce, thinly sliced

1 tablespoon olive oil

1 tablespoon cider vinegar

1/2 teaspoon coarsely ground pepper

1/4 teaspoon salt

1. Prepare outdoor grill for covered direct grilling over medium-high heat.

2. Place corn on hot grill rack over medium-high heat. Cover grill and cook corn, turning frequently, until brown in spots, 10 to 15 minutes.

3. Transfer corn to plate; set aside until cool enough to handle. When cool, with sharp knife, cut kernels from cobs.

4. Place tortillas on work surface. Evenly divide Monterey Jack, salsa, green onions, and corn on half of each tortilla. Fold tortilla over filling to make 4 quesadillas.

5. Place quesadillas on hot grill rack. Grill quesadillas, turning once, until they are browned on both sides, 1 to 2 minutes. Transfer quesadillas to cutting board; cut each into 3 pieces.

6. In large bowl, toss romaine with oil, vinegar, pepper, and salt. Serve quesadillas with romaine salad.

Each serving: About 330 calories, 16g protein, 47g carbohydrate, 11g total fat (5g saturated), 20mg cholesterol, 940mg sodium.

Corn and Jack Quesadillas

Charred-Corn and Bean Salad

A fresh mix of sweet corn, red onion, and pinto beans is tossed with a south-of-the-border zesty vinaigrette.

PREP: 25 MINUTES   GRILL: 10 TO 15 MINUTES
MAKES 6 ACCOMPANIMENT SERVINGS

3 medium ears corn, husks and silk
  removed
1 small red onion, cut into 4 slices
1 can (15 to 19 ounces) pinto or
  small pink beans, rinsed and
  drained
1 jalapeño chile, seeded and minced

1/2 cup loosely packed fresh cilantro
  leaves, chopped
3 tablespoons fresh lime juice
1 tablespoon olive oil
3/4 teaspoon salt
1/4 teaspoon coarsely ground black
  pepper

1. Prepare outdoor grill for direct grilling over medium-high heat.

2. Place corn and onion slices on hot grill rack over medium-high heat. Grill corn, turning occasionally until golden, 10 to 15 minutes. Grill onion, turning once, until tender and golden, 10 minutes.

3. Transfer vegetables to cutting board. Cut corn kernels from cobs and chop onion. In large bowl, mix corn and onion with beans, jalapeño, cilantro, lime juice, oil, salt, and pepper. Cover and refrigerate if not serving right away.

Each serving: About 140 calories, 6g protein, 25g carbohydrate, 3g total fat (0g saturated), 0mg cholesterol, 500mg sodium.

Grilled Polenta with Fontina

This easy side dish begins with slices of precooked polenta from the supermarket. We added melted cheese and chopped tomatoes for a tasty topping. Precooked polenta comes in a log shape and may be found in the dairy section of your supermarket.

PREP: 10 MINUTES   GRILL: ABOUT 10 MINUTES
MAKES 6 ACCOMPANIMENT SERVINGS

2 ripe medium tomatoes (about 12 ounces), chopped
2 tablespoons chopped fresh parsley
1/4 teaspoon salt
1/8 teaspoon coarsely ground black pepper

1 package (24 ounces) precooked polenta, cut into 12 slices
1 tablespoon olive oil
2 ounces Fontina cheese, shredded (1/2 cup)

1. Prepare outdoor grill for direct grilling over medium heat.
2. In small bowl, combine tomatoes, parsley, salt, and pepper; set aside.
3. Brush both sides of polenta slices with olive oil. Place polenta slices on hot grill rack over medium heat and grill until undersides are golden, 5 minutes. Turn slices and top with Fontina cheese. Grill polenta just until cheese melts, about 5 minutes longer.
4. Transfer polenta slices to platter and top with tomato mixture.

Each serving: About 150 calories, 5g protein, 19g carbohydrate, 5g total fat (2g saturated), 11mg cholesterol, 380mg sodium.

TIP: Can't find Fontina? Substitute Monterey Jack or Muenster cheese. If you'd like to save time, top the grilled polenta with a drizzle of store-bought pesto or salsa instead of our fresh tomato topping.

Grilled Eggplant Parmesan

Grilling gives eggplant a smoky flavor, and eliminating the frying makes this outdoor version of Eggplant Parmesan light and fresh tasting. Use freshly grated Parmesan cheese and the ripest summer tomatoes you can find for this flavorful variation on the traditional dish.

PREP: 25 MINUTES   GRILL: 9 TO 12 MINUTES   MAKES 4 SERVINGS

1 medium-large eggplant (about
    1 1/2 pounds), cut lengthwise
    into 4 slices
1 tablespoon plus 1 teaspoon olive oil
1/2 teaspoon salt
1/4 teaspoon coarsely ground black
    pepper

4 ounces mozzarella cheese,
    shredded (1 cup)
1/4 cup grated Parmesan cheese
1/2 cup loosely packed fresh basil
    leaves, sliced
2 medium ripe tomatoes, each cut
    into 4 slices

1. Prepare outdoor grill for covered direct grilling over medium heat.

2. Lightly brush eggplant slices with oil and sprinkle with salt and pepper. In small bowl, mix mozzarella, Parmesan, and basil; set aside.

3. Place eggplant slices on hot grill rack over medium heat and grill, turning once, until tender and lightly browned, 8 to 10 minutes. Top eggplant slices with tomato slices and cheese mixture. Cover grill and cook until cheese melts and tomato slices are warm, 1 to 2 minutes.

Each serving: About 205 calories, 10g protein, 15g carbohydrate, 13g total fat (5g saturated), 26mg cholesterol, 500mg sodium.

TIP: Look for an eggplant that is firm, without any soft brown spots.

Grilled Eggplant Parmesan

Mediterranean Grilled Eggplant and Summer Squash

This recipe doubles easily; if you're feeding a crowd, grill the vegetables in batches. Ricotta salata is a firm, white, lightly salted cheese made ftom sheep's milk. Look for it in supermarkets, cheese shops, and Italian groceries.

PREP: 15 MINUTES   GRILL: 10 TO 15 MINUTES
MAKES 6 ACCOMPANIMENT SERVINGS

3 tablespoons olive oil

2 tablespoons red wine vinegar

2 teaspoons Dijon mustard

1/4 teaspoon salt

1/4 teaspoon coarsely ground black pepper

1 garlic clove, crushed with garlic press

1 medium zucchini (about 8 ounces), cut lengthwise into 1/4-inch-thick slices

1 medium yellow squash (about 8 ounces), cut lengthwise into 1/4-inch-thick slices

1 small eggplant (about 1 1/4 pounds), cut lengthwise into 1/4-inch-thick slices

2 tablespoons chopped fresh mint

1 ounce crumbled ricotta salata or feta cheese (1/4 cup)

1. Prepare outdoor grill for direct grilling over medium heat.

2. Prepare vinaigrette: In small bowl, with wire whisk, mix oil, vinegar, mustard, salt, pepper, and garlic.

3. Brush one side of each vegetable slice with some vinaigrette. Place vegetables on hot grill rack over medium heat and grill, turning once and brushing with remaining vinaigrette, until vegetables are browned and tender, 10 to 15 minutes.

4. Transfer vegetables to large platter as they are done. Sprinkle with mint and ricotta salata.

Each serving: About 115 calories, 3g protein, 9g carbohydrate, 8g total fat (2g saturated), 4mg cholesterol, 220mg sodium.

TIP: Grilled vegetables make a wonderful sandwich. Fill sliced crusty Italian bread with vegetables and extra cheese.

Glazed Japanese Eggplant

Make sure you buy Japanese eggplants for this recipe—they're purple and usually long and slender. Delicious either hot off the grill, chilled, or at room temperature. For an added touch, sprinkle the eggplants with toasted sesame seeds just before serving.

PREP: 15 MINUTES   GRILL: ABOUT 10 MINUTES
MAKES 6 ACCOMPANIMENT SERVINGS

6 medium Japanese eggplants (about 5 ounces each), each cut lengthwise in half
1 tablespoon dark brown sugar
1 tablespoon minced, peeled fresh ginger
3 tablespoons soy sauce
1 tablespoon seasoned rice vinegar
1/2 teaspoon Asian sesame oil
1/4 teaspoon cornstarch
3 garlic cloves, crushed with garlic press
3 tablespoons water
4 teaspoons vegetable oil

1. Prepare outdoor grill for direct grilling over medium heat.

2. With knife, score cut side of each eggplant half with several 1/4-inch-deep parallel diagonal slits, being careful not to cut through to skin. Repeat with second set of slits perpendicular to first to form diamond pattern.

3. In small bowl, with fork, mix brown sugar, ginger, soy sauce, vinegar, sesame oil, cornstarch, garlic, and water.

4. Brush cut side of eggplant halves with vegetable oil. With tongs, place eggplant halves, cut side down, on hot grill rack over medium heat and grill until lightly browned, about 5 minutes.

5. Fold 30" by 18" sheet of heavy-duty foil crosswise in half. Place grilled eggplant halves on double thickness of foil. Pour soy-sauce mixture over eggplant halves, bring long sides of foil up, and fold several times to seal. Fold over ends to seal in juices.

6. Place foil packet on grill rack over medium heat and cook until eggplant is soft, about 5 minutes.

7. Before serving, with kitchens shears, cut an X in top of foil packet to let steam escape, then carefully pull back foil to open. To serve, lift out eggplant, and spoon any juices over.

Each serving: About 85 calories, 2g protein, 13g carbohydrate, 4g total fat (0g saturated), 0mg cholesterol, 570mg sodium.

Grilled Eggplant, Peppers, Zucchini, and Summer Squash

Great served hot or at room temperature. Double the amounts if serving a crowd, and cook the vegetables in batches. Add some French bread slices to grill alongside the veggies, if you like.

PREP: 15 MINUTES   GRILL: ABOUT 7 MINUTES
MAKES 8 ACCOMPANIMENT SERVINGS

3 tablespoons olive oil
2 tablespoons red wine vinegar
1/4 teaspoon salt
1/4 teaspoon coarsely ground black pepper
1/4 cup loosely packed fresh basil leaves, coarsely chopped
1 medium red pepper cut lengthwise into quarters, stem and seeds discarded

1 medium yellow pepper cut lengthwise into quarters, stem and seeds discarded
4 baby eggplants (about 5 ounces each), each cut lengthwise in half
4 small zucchini and/or yellow summer squash (about 6 ounces each), each cut lengthwise in half

1. Prepare outdoor grill for covered direct grilling over medium-high heat.
2. Meanwhile, in cup, mix oil, vinegar, salt, pepper, and basil.
3. Place peppers, eggplant, zucchini and squash on hot grill rack over medium-high heat. Cover grill and cook vegetables, turning and brushing with herb mixture occasionally and transferring vegetables to platter as they are done, until tender and browned, 7 to 10 minutes.
4. Drizzle vegetables with any remaining herb mixture and serve.

Each serving: About 80 calories, 2g protein, 8g carbohydrate, 5g total fat (1g saturated), 0mg cholesterol, 75mg sodium.

Grilled Eggplant, Peppers,
Zucchini, and Summer Squash

Chili Potato Packet

We turned up the heat with ground red pepper, onion, and chili powder for Tex-Mex appeal. To jazz it up even further, toss the grilled potatoes with cooked corn kernels, fresh lime juice, chopped cilantro, and shredded Monterey Jack cheese.

PREP: 15 MINUTES   GRILL: 30 MINUTES
MAKES 8 ACCOMPANIMENT SERVINGS

2 1/2 pounds red potatoes, not
  peeled and cut into 1-inch chunks
1 large red pepper, cut into 1-inch
  pieces
1 medium onion, coarsely chopped

2 tablespoons olive oil
1 tablespoon chili powder
1 teaspoon salt
1/4 teaspoon ground red pepper
  (cayenne)

1. Prepare outdoor grill for covered direct grilling over medium heat.

2. In large bowl, toss potatoes, red pepper, onion, oil, chili powder, salt, and ground red pepper until potatoes are evenly coated.

3. Layer two 30" by 18" sheets heavy-duty foil to make double-thick sheet. Place potato mixture in center of stacked foil. Bring short ends of foil up and over potatoes; fold several times to seal. Fold remaining sides of foil several times to seal in juices.

4. Place packet on hot grill rack over medium heat and cook, turning packet over once halfway through grilling, until potatoes are fork-tender, about 30 minutes.

5. Before serving, with kitchen shears, cut an X in top of foil packet to let steam escape, then carefully pull back foil to open.

Each serving: About 145 calories, 4g protein, 26g carbohydrate, 4g total fat (1g saturated), 0mg cholesterol, 285mg sodium.

TIP: Try substituting peeled and cut sweet potatoes for the red potatoes and use a green pepper in place of the red.

Rosemary Potato Packet

Grated orange peel adds a hint of sweetness to these lightly spiced spuds. Look for foil cooking bags in your supermarket where foil and plastic wrap are sold.

PREP: 15 MINUTES   GRILL: ABOUT 30 MINUTES
MAKES 8 ACCOMPANIMENT SERVINGS

2 1/2 pounds red potatoes, not peeled and cut into 1-inch chunks
1 tablespoon olive oil
1 tablespoon fresh rosemary leaves, chopped
1 teaspoon grated orange peel
1 teaspoon salt
1/4 teaspoon coarsely ground black pepper

1. Prepare outdoor grill for covered direct grilling over medium heat.
2. In large bowl, toss potatoes, oil, rosemary, orange peel, salt, and pepper until potatoes are evenly coated.
3. Layer two 30" by 18" sheets heavy-duty foil to make double-thick sheet. Place potato mixture in center of stacked foil. Bring short ends of foil up and over potatoes; fold several times to seal. Fold remaining sides of foil several times to seal in juices.
4. Place packet on hot grill rack over medium heat. Cover grill and cook, turning packet over once halfway through grilling, until potatoes are fork-tender, about 30 minutes.
5. Before serving, with kitchen shears, cut an X in top of foil packet to let steam escape, then carefully pull back foil to open.

Each serving: About 135 calories, 3g protein, 28g carbohydrate, 2g total fat (0g saturated), 0mg cholesterol, 300mg sodium.

Lemon-Garlic Potato Packet

Lemon-Garlic Potato Packet

Whole cloves of garlic grill up butter-soft along with the potatoes. If you like, once the potatoes and garlic are cooked (and while they're still warm), toss them with your favorite vinaigrette for a grilled potato salad.

PREP: 15 MINUTES   GRILL: 30 MINUTES
MAKES 8 ACCOMPANIMENT SERVINGS

2 1/2 pounds red potatoes, not
   peeled and cut into 1-inch chunks
12 garlic cloves, peeled
2 tablespoons olive oil

1 1/2 teaspoons freshly grated
   lemon peel
1 teaspoon salt
1/4 teaspoon coarsely ground
   black pepper

1. Prepare outdoor grill for covered direct grilling over medium heat.

2. In large bowl, toss potatoes, garlic, oil, lemon peel, salt, and pepper until potatoes are evenly coated.

3. Layer two 30" by 18" sheets heavy-duty foil to make double-thick sheet. Place potato mixture in center of stacked foil. Bring short ends of foil up and over potatoes; fold several times to seal. Fold remaining sides of foil several times to seal in juices.

4. Place packet on hot grill rack over medium heat and cook, turning packet over once halfway through grilling, until potatoes are fork-tender, 30 minutes.

5. Before serving, with kitchen shears, cut an X in top of foil packet to let steam escape, then carefully pull back foil to open.

Each serving: About 140 calories, 3g protein, 25g carbohydrate, 4g total fat (1g saturated), 0mg cholesterol, 275mg sodium.

Shallot and Herb Potato Packet

Prepare as directed but omit garlic. Add *2 medium shallots*, thinly sliced, and *2 teaspoons minced fresh thyme* or *1/2 teaspoon dried thyme*. Wrap and grill as directed. Sprinkle with *1/3 cup chopped fresh parsley* before serving.

Each serving: About 140 calories, 3g protein, 25g carbohydrate, 4g total fat (1g saturated), 0mg cholesterol, 280mg sodium.

Crumb-Topped Tomatoes

You can't get the bread crumbs crusty on the grill, so brown them ahead of time in a skillet. The crumbs may be prepared up to a day ahead and refrigerated. These would make the perfect accompaniment to Grilled Halibut with Fresh Dill (page 152) or Red Wine and Rosemary Porterhouse (page 96).

PREP: 15 MINUTES   GRILL: 8 TO 10 MINUTES
MAKES 8 ACCOMPANIMENT SERVINGS

2 tablespoons butter or margarine
1 cup fresh bread crumbs (about
  2 slices firm white bread)
1 garlic clove, crushed with garlic
  press
2 tablespoons chopped fresh parsley
  leaves

1/2 teaspoon salt
1/2 teaspoon coarsely ground black
  pepper
8 large ripe plum tomatoes

1. Prepare outdoor grill for direct grilling over medium heat.

2. In 10-inch skillet, melt butter over low heat. Add bread crumbs and cook, stirring, until lightly browned. Stir in garlic; cook 30 seconds. Remove skillet from heat; stir in parsley, salt, and pepper.

3. Cut each tomato horizontally in half. Top each tomato half with some crumb mixture. Place tomatoes on hot grill rack over medium heat and grill until hot but not mushy, 8 to 10 minutes.

Each serving: About 40 calories, 1g protein, 3g carbohydrate, 3g total fat (2g saturated), 8mg cholesterol, 191mg sodium.

TIP: To make fresh bread crumbs, tear bread into large pieces and process the pieces in a food processor with the knife blade attached to form crumbs. For dried bread crumbs, cut stale bread into large chunks and process the chunks in a food processor to form crumbs. Store the crumbs in ziptight plastic bags and freeze until needed.

Vegetarian Burritos

To make this all-in-one entrée, roll grilled onion, peppers, and zucchini in tortillas with shredded cheeses. If you prefer your burritos mild, substitute Monterey Jack without jalapeño chiles or use all Cheddar cheese. Serve with your favorite bottled salsa and a dollop of sour cream. Burritos may be cut into bite-size portions and served as appetizers.

PREP: 25 MINUTES GRILL: 16 TO 21 MINUTES MAKES 4 SERVINGS

1 tablespoon plus 1 teaspoon vegetable oil
1 teaspoon chili powder
1 teaspoon ground cumin
1/2 teaspoon salt
1/4 teaspoon coarsely ground black pepper
2 medium zucchini (about 10 ounces each), each cut lengthwise into 1/4-inch-thick slices
1 large onion, cut into 1/2-inch-thick slices
1 medium red pepper, quartered, stem and seeds discarded
1 medium green pepper, quartered, stem and seeds discarded
4 (10-inch) flour tortillas
1/2 cup shredded sharp Cheddar cheese (2 ounces)
1/2 cup shredded Monterey Jack cheese with jalapeño chiles (2 ounces)
1/2 cup packed fresh cilantro leaves
bottled salsa (optional)

1. Prepare outdoor grill for covered direct grilling over medium heat.
2. In small bowl, mix vegetable oil, chili powder, cumin, salt, and black pepper. Brush one side of zucchini slices, onion slices, and pepper pieces with oil mixture.
3. Place vegetables, oiled side down, on hot grill rack over medium heat and grill, turning once, and transferring vegetables to plate as they are done, until tender and golden, 15 to 20 minutes.
4. Arrange one-fourth of grilled vegetables down center of each tortilla; sprinkle with Cheddar and Monterey Jack cheeses. Place open burritos on grill rack. Cover grill and cook until cheeses melt, about 1 minute.
5. Transfer burritos to plates. Sprinkle cilantro over cheese, then fold sides of tortillas over filling. Serve with salsa, if you like.

Each serving: About 330 calories, 11g protein, 43g carbohydrate, 14g total fat (4g saturated), 15mg cholesterol, 655mg sodium.

Grilled Vegetables Vinaigrette

Serve these vegetables as an accompaniment to any grilled meat, poultry, or seafood. For a delightful summer salad, cut the grilled vegetables into bite-size pieces and toss them with potatoes from Lemon-Garlic Potato Packets (page 201) or from one of the other grilled potato packets.

PREP: 15 MINUTES   GRILL: 10 TO 15 MINUTES
MAKES 8 ACCOMPANIMENT SERVINGS

1/2 cup olive oil
1/2 cup white wine vinegar
8 teaspoons chopped fresh tarragon
1 1/2 teaspoons salt
1 1/2 teaspoons coarsely ground black pepper
1 teaspoon sugar
2 medium yellow peppers, halved lengthwise, stem and seeds discarded

2 medium red peppers, halved lengthwise, stem and seeds discarded
4 small zucchini (about 6 ounces each), halved lengthwise
4 baby eggplants (about 4 ounces each), halved lengthwise
2 medium portobello mushrooms (about 4 ounces each), stems removed

1. Prepare outdoor grill for direct grilling over medium heat.

2. Prepare vinaigrette: In large bowl, with wire whisk, mix oil, vinegar, tarragon, salt, pepper, and sugar. Add yellow and red peppers, zucchini, eggplants, and mushrooms to bowl; toss to coat.

3. Place yellow and red peppers, zucchini, eggplant, and mushrooms on hot grill rack over medium heat and grill, turning vegetables occasionally and brushing with some remaining vinaigrette, until vegetables are browned and tender when pierced with a fork, 10 to 15 minutes.

4. Once vegetables are cooked, cut each portobello into quarters. Serve vegetables with remaining vinaigrette.

Each serving: About 170 calories, 3g protein, 11g carbohydrate, 14g total fat (2g saturated), 0mg cholesterol, 445mg sodium.

TIP: Going to a picnic? You can grill the vegetables, toss them with the vinaigrette, and carry them along.

Grilled Vegetables Vinaigrette

Grilled Tofu and Veggies

A great hoisin-ginger glaze flavors tofu, zucchini, and red pepper. Be sure to buy extra-firm tofu; other varieties will fall apart while cooking.

PREP: 25 MINUTES   GRILL: ABOUT 11 MINUTES   MAKES 4 SERVINGS

HOISIN-GINGER GLAZE
- 1/2 cup hoisin sauce
- 2 garlic cloves, crushed with garlic press
- 1 tablespoon vegetable oil
- 1 tablespoon reduced-sodium soy sauce
- 1 tablespoon grated, peeled fresh ginger
- 1 tablespoon seasoned rice vinegar
- 1/8 teaspoon ground red pepper (cayenne)

TOFU AND VEGGIES
- 1 package (15 ounces) extra-firm tofu
- 2 medium zucchini (about 10 ounces each), each cut lengthwise into quarters and then crosswise in half
- 1 large red pepper, cut lengthwise into quarters, stem and seeds discarded
- 1 bunch green onions, trimmed
- 1 teaspoon vegetable oil

1. Prepare outdoor grill for direct grilling over medium heat.

2. Prepare glaze: In small bowl, with fork, mix hoisin sauce, garlic, oil, soy sauce, ginger, vinegar, and ground red pepper until well blended.

3. Prepare tofu and veggies: Cut tofu horizontally into 4 pieces, then cut each piece crosswise in half. Place tofu on paper towels; pat dry with additional paper towels. Arrange tofu on large plate and brush both sides of tofu with half of glaze. Spoon remaining half of glaze into medium bowl; add zucchini and red pepper. Gently toss vegetables to coat with glaze. On another plate, rub green onions with oil.

4. Place tofu, zucchini, and red peppers on hot grill rack over medium heat and grill tofu, gently turning once with wide metal spatula, 6 minutes. Transfer tofu to platter; keep warm. Continue cooking vegetables, transferring them to platter with tofu as they are done, until tender and browned, about 5 minutes longer.

5. Add green onions to grill rack during last minute of cooking time; transfer to platter.

Each serving: About 245 calories, 15g protein, 22g carbohydrate, 11g total fat (1g saturated), 0mg cholesterol, 615mg sodium.

Veggie Kabobs

A slightly sweet balsamic vinaigrette adds zip to an assortment of colorful vegetables. For added variety, thread large mushroom caps and wedges of red onion onto the skewers with the other vegetables. Prepare extra vinaigrette and additional skewers.

PREP: 15 MINUTES   GRILL: 15 TO 20 MINUTES
MAKES 6 ACCOMPANIMENT SERVINGS

3 small zucchini (about 6 ounces each), cut diagonally into 1-inch chunks

3 small yellow summer squash (about 6 ounces each), cut diagonally into 1-inch chunks

6 ripe plum tomatoes (about 1 1/4 pounds), each cut lengthwise in half

1 tablespoon brown sugar

1 tablespoon balsamic vinegar

1/2 teaspoon salt

1/8 teaspoon coarsely ground black pepper

1/8 teaspoon ground cinnamon

3 tablespoons olive oil

3/4 cup loosely packed fresh basil leaves, thinly sliced

6 (12-inch) metal skewers

1. Prepare outdoor grill for direct grilling over medium heat.

2. Alternately thread zucchini chunks, yellow squash chunks, and tomato halves onto metal skewers, leaving about 1/8-inch space between each vegetable piece. (Threading zucchini and squash through skin side gives vegetables more stability on skewers.)

3. In cup, combine brown sugar, vinegar, salt, pepper, cinnamon, and 2 tablespoons olive oil. Brush kabobs with remaining 1 tablespoon oil.

4. Place kabobs on hot grill rack over medium heat and grill, turning kabobs occasionally and brushing vegetables with some vinaigrette during last 3 minutes of cooking, until vegetables are browned and tender, 15 to 20 minutes.

5. To serve, arrange kabobs on large platter; drizzle with any remaining vinaigrette and sprinkle with basil.

Each serving: About 120 calories, 3g protein, 13g carbohydrate, 7g total fat (1g saturated), 0mg cholesterol, 210mg sodium.

Hot Fruit Salad

Hot Fruit Salad

A few turns on the grill transform fresh fruit into a sumptuous finale.

PREP: 15 MINUTES   GRILL: 10 TO 15 MINUTES   MAKES 6 SERVINGS

1/2 cup honey
1 tablespoon fresh lemon juice
1/4 cup loosely packed fresh mint
  leaves, thinly sliced
1 medium pineapple, cut lengthwise
  into 6 wedges, with leaves
  attached

2 large bananas, each cut diagonally
  into thirds
3 medium plums, each cut in half
  and pitted
2 medium nectarines or peaches,
  each cut into quarters and pitted

1. Prepare outdoor grill for direct grilling over medium heat.
2. In cup, stir honey, lemon juice, and 1 tablespoon mint leaves.
3. With tongs, place fruit pieces on hot grill rack over medium heat and grill, turning fruit occasionally and brushing fruit with honey mixture during last 3 minutes of cooking, until browned and tender, 10 to 15 minutes.
4. To serve, arrange grilled fruit on large platter; drizzle with any remaining honey mixture. Sprinkle grilled fruit with remaining mint.

Each serving: About 215 calories, 2g protein, 55g carbohydrate, 1g total fat (0g saturated), 0mg cholesterol, 5mg sodium.

Toasted Angel Cake

Serve golden wedges of cake with sun-ripened berries and brown-sugar whipped cream. Try with grilled pound cake slices too!

PREP: 10 MINUTES   GRILL: ABOUT 1 MINUTE   MAKES 6 SERVINGS

1 pint strawberries, hulled and each cut into quarters
1 cup blueberries
3 tablespoons light brown sugar
1/2 cup heavy or whipping cream
1 teaspoon vanilla extract
1 store-bought angel food cake (12 ounces)

1. Prepare outdoor grill for direct grilling over medium heat.
2. In medium bowl, toss strawberries and blueberries with 1 tablespoon brown sugar to coat; set aside.
3. In small bowl, with mixer at medium speed, beat cream and vanilla until soft peaks form when beaters are lifted. Gradually add remaining 2 tablespoons brown sugar and beat until stiff peaks form. Cover and refrigerate.
4. Cut cake into 6 wedges. Place cake on hot grill rack over medium heat and toast, turning once, until golden on both sides, about 1 minute.
5. To serve, place cake on dessert plates; top each wedge with berry mixture, then a dollop of whipped cream.

Each serving: About 270 calories, 4g protein, 47g carbohydrate, 8g total fat (5g saturated), 27mg cholesterol, 435mg sodium.

TIP: Raspberries, blackberries, nectarines, and apricots all are delicious in this recipe. Allow about 1/2 cup prepared fruit per person.

Toasted Angel Cake

RUBS, SAUCES & SALSAS

(From left) Asian Salsa, Southwest Corn Salsa, Tomato and Lemon Salsa, Mango and Red Pepper Salsa

Lime-Herb Rub

Use this for our Mixed Grill with Asian Flavors (page 140). It's also great rubbed under the skin of a chicken, over a pork tenderloin, or on salmon or other oily fish.

PREP: 15 MINUTES   MAKES ABOUT 1 1/2 CUPS

2 limes
2 cups loosely packed fresh cilantro
  leaves, chopped
2 cups loosely packed fresh mint
  leaves, chopped
2 tablespoons brown sugar
2 tablespoons minced, peeled fresh
  ginger

3 garlic cloves, crushed with garlic
  press
2 green onions, thinly sliced
2 teaspoons salt
1 teaspoon crushed red pepper

1. From limes, grate 1 tablespoon peel and squeeze 2 tablespoons juice.
2. In medium bowl, combine lime peel, lime juice, cilantro, mint, sugar, ginger, garlic, green onions, salt, and crushed red pepper. Use rub right away.

Each 1/3 cup: About 70 calories, 3g protein, 16g carbohydrate, 1g total fat (0g saturated), 0mg cholesterol, 1,195mg sodium.

Salt-Free Herb Rub

Our crush of dried herbs may earn your saltshaker a well-deserved summer vacation. Try it on grilled pork or fish.

PREP: 5 MINUTES   MAKES ABOUT ¹/₄ CUP

2 tablespoons dried rosemary
2 tablespoons dried thyme
1 tablespoon dried tarragon

1 tablespoon coarsely ground black pepper

In mortar with pestle, or with fingers, crush together rosemary, thyme, tarragon, and pepper. Use 2 teaspoons herb mixture per pound of uncooked beef or pork; 1 teaspoon per pound of uncooked fish or chicken. Store in tightly covered container and use within 6 months.

Each teaspoon: About 5 calories, 0g protein, 1g carbohydrate, 0g total fat (0g saturated), 0mg cholesterol, 1mg sodium.

Spicy Peppercorn Rub

Our simple salt-free blend works well for steak, pork, chicken, or lamb. We like to pat about 2 tablespoons on a 1- to 2-pound steak—you can use more or less, depending on the meat's thickness.

PREP: 10 MINUTES   MAKES ABOUT ¹/₂ CUP

3 tablespoons coriander seeds
3 tablespoons cumin seeds
3 tablespoons fennel seeds

1 tablespoon whole black
   peppercorns

Spoon coriander seeds, cumin seeds, fennel seeds, and black peppercorns into ziptight plastic bag. Place kitchen towel over bag and, with meat mallet or rolling pin, coarsely crush spices. Rub desired amount all over steak(s) before grilling. If not using right away, store rub in tightly sealed container in cool, dry place up to 2 months.

Each tablespoon: About 25 calories, 2g protein, 4g carbohydrate, 1g total fat (0g saturated), 0mg cholesterol, 7mg sodium.

Cajun Rub

This spicy mix gives chops or chicken breasts a yummy crust.

PREP: 5 MINUTES   MAKES ABOUT 1/3 CUP

2 tablespoons paprika
1 tablespoon coarsely ground black
  pepper
1 tablespoon ground cumin
1 tablespoon brown sugar
1 tablespoon salt
2 teaspoons ground coriander

1 teaspoon dried thyme
1 teaspoon ground red pepper
  (cayenne)
1/2 teaspoon garlic powder
1/2 teaspoon ground allspice

In small bowl, mix paprika, black pepper, cumin, brown sugar, salt, coriander, thyme, ground red pepper, garlic powder, and allspice. Use 1 tablespoon spice mixture per pound of uncooked beef or pork; 2 teaspoons per pound of uncooked fish or chicken. Store in tightly covered container and use within 6 months.

Each tablespoon: About 26 calories, 1g protein, 5g carbohydrate, 1g total fat (0g saturated), 0mg cholesterol, 1,400mg sodium.

French Tarragon Rub

This rub has all the lucious flavor but none of the fat of a rich béarnaise sauce.

PREP: 10 MINUTES   MAKES ABOUT 1/2 CUP

2 medium shallots, minced (1/4 cup)

2 tablespoons red wine vinegar

1 tablespoon dried tarragon

1 teaspoon salt

1/2 teaspoon coarsely ground black pepper

In cup, stir together shallots, vinegar, tarragon, salt, and pepper. Rub full amount all over meat or chicken before grilling.

Each tablespoon: About 6 calories, 0g protein, 1g carbohydrate, 0g total fat (0g saturated), 0mg cholesterol, 292mg sodium.

Chunky BBQ Sauce

Good on pork or chicken. Refrigerate up to one week or freeze up to two months.

PREP: 10 MINUTES   COOK: 17 TO 18 MINUTES   MAKES ABOUT 4 CUPS

1 tablespoon vegetable oil
1 large onion, chopped
3 garlic cloves, minced
2 tablespoons minced, peeled fresh ginger
1 teaspoon ground cumin
1 can (14 1/2 ounces) tomatoes in puree, chopped, puree reserved

1 bottle (12 ounces) chili sauce
1/3 cup cider vinegar
2 tablespoons brown sugar
2 tablespoons light (mild) molasses
2 teaspoons dry mustard
1 tablespoon cornstarch
2 tablespoons water

1. In 12-inch skillet, heat oil over medium heat until hot. Add onion and cook, stirring occasionally, until tender, about 10 minutes. Add garlic and ginger and cook, stirring, 1 minute. Stir in cumin.

2. Stir in tomatoes, reserved puree, chili sauce, vinegar, brown sugar, molasses, and dry mustard; heat to boiling over high heat. Reduce heat to medium-high and cook, uncovered, 5 minutes, stirring occasionally.

3. In cup, mix cornstarch and water until blended. Stir mixture into sauce and cook until sauce boils and thickens, 1 to 2 minutes longer. Cover and refrigerate if not using right away.

Each 1/2 cup: About 120 calories, 2g protein, 25g carbohydrate, 2g total fat (0g saturated), 0mg cholesterol, 655mg sodium.

Secret-Recipe BBQ Sauce

Pineapple adds tang to this slow-simmered sauce. Brush it over anything from hamburgers to chicken.

PREP: 15 MINUTES   COOK: 40 MINUTES   MAKES ABOUT 5 CUPS

1 tablespoon olive oil
1 large onion (12 ounces), chopped
2 tablespoons chopped, peeled fresh
  ginger
3 tablespoons chili powder
3 garlic cloves, crushed with garlic
  press
1 can (8 ounces) crushed pineapple
  in juice

1 can (28 ounces) crushed tomatoes
  in puree
1/3 cup ketchup
1/4 cup cider vinegar
3 tablespoons dark brown sugar
3 tablespoons light (mild) molasses
2 teaspoons dry mustard
1 teaspoon salt

1. In 5- to 6-quart saucepot, heat olive oil over medium heat until hot. (Do not use a smaller pan; sauce bubbles up and splatters during cooking—the deeper the pan, the better.) Add onion and ginger; cook until onion is tender and golden, about 10 minutes. Add chili powder; cook, stirring, 1 minute. Add garlic and crushed pineapple with its juice, and cook 1 minute longer.

2. Remove pot from heat. Stir in tomatoes with their puree, ketchup, vinegar, brown sugar, molasses, dry mustard, and salt. Spoon one-fourth of sauce into blender. At low speed, puree until smooth. Pour sauce into bowl; repeat with remaining sauce.

3. Return sauce to saucepot; heat to boiling over high heat. Reduce heat to medium-low and cook, partially covered, stirring occasionally, until reduced to about 5 cups, about 25 minutes.

4. Cover and refrigerate if not using right away. Sauce will keep up to 1 week in refrigerator or up to 2 months in freezer.

Each cup: About 220 calories, 3g protein, 47g carbohydrate, 3g total fat (0g saturated), 0mg cholesterol, 960mg sodium.

Chimichurri Sauce

This tasty green sauce, thick with fresh herbs, is as common in Argentina as ketchup is in the United States. It can be prepared ahead and refrigerated up to two days. Great drizzled over meat and poultry—or tossed with hot cooked pasta. You can even use it as a salad dressing.

PREP: 15 MINUTES   MAKES ABOUT 1/2 CUP

1 1/2 cups loosely packed fresh
   parsley leaves, finely chopped
1 1/2 cups loosely packed fresh
   cilantro leaves, finely chopped
1/4 cup olive oil
3 tablespoons red wine vinegar

1 garlic clove, crushed with garlic
   press
1/4 teaspoon coarsely ground black
   pepper
1/4 teaspoon salt

In small bowl, mix parsley, cilantro, oil, vinegar, garlic, pepper, and salt. Cover and refrigerate if not using right away.

Each tablespoon: About 65 calories, 0g protein, 1g carbohydrate, 7g total fat (1g saturated), 0mg cholesterol, 70mg sodium.

Guacamole

Great with Steak Fajitas with Guacamole (page 109), grilled pork, or grilled chicken, or as a topper for Grilled Flatbread (page 19).

Prep: 20 minutes   Makes about 3 cups

2 medium ripe avocados (about 8 ounces each), peeled, pitted, and cut into 1-inch chunks
2 ripe medium tomatoes (about 10 ounces), coarsely chopped
1 jalapeño chile, seeded and minced

1 cup loosely packed fresh cilantro leaves, chopped
1 tablespoon fresh lime juice
1/2 teaspoon salt

In medium bowl, gently stir avocados, tomatoes, jalapeño, cilantro, lime juice, and salt until mixed. Cover with plastic wrap and refrigerate if not serving right away.

Each tablespoon: About 15 calories, 0g protein, 1g carbohydrate, 1g total fat (0g saturated), 0mg cholesterol, 25mg sodium.

Pineapple Salsa

Spiked with jalapeño and cilantro, this spicy-sweet fruit salsa turns simply grilled fish, pork, and chicken into a sensational meal.

PREP: 15 MINUTES   MAKES ABOUT 4 CUPS

2 limes
1 ripe pineapple (rind removed),
    cored and coarsely chopped
1 cup loosely packed fresh cilantro
    leaves, chopped
1 jalapeño chile, seeded and minced

1 green onion, sliced
1 teaspoon sugar
1/4 teaspoon salt
1/8 teaspoon coarsely ground black
    pepper

1. From limes, grate $1/2$ teaspoon peel and squeeze 2 tablespoons juice.
2. In medium bowl, mix lime peel and juice with pineapple, cilantro, jalapeño, green onion, sugar, salt, and pepper. Cover and refrigerate until ready to serve.

Each 1/4 cup: About 20 calories, 0g protein, 5g carbohydrate, 0g total fat (0g saturated), 0mg cholesterol, 35mg sodium.

Mango Salsa

The combination of mango and kiwifruit gives this salsa its sweet and tangy flavor. Try substituting chopped pitted fresh cherries and a diced yellow pepper for the mango and kiwifruit.

PREP: 15 MINUTES   MAKES ABOUT 4 CUPS

2 ripe medium mangoes, peeled, pitted and coarsely chopped
2 medium kiwifruit, peeled and coarsely chopped
3 tablespoons seasoned rice vinegar

1 tablespoon grated, peeled fresh ginger
1 tablespoon minced fresh cilantro leaves

In medium bowl, combine mangoes, kiwifruit, rice vinegar, ginger, and cilantro. Cover and refrigerate if not serving right away.

Each 1/4 cup: About 25 calories, 0g protein, 6g carbohydrate, 0g total fat (0g saturated), 0mg cholesterol, 60mg sodium.

Melon Salsa

Serve with Pepper-Rubbed Salmon (page 163) or try it with grilled pork or poultry.

PREP: 15 MINUTES   MAKES ABOUT 4 CUPS

2 cups (1/4-inch dice) cantaloupe
2 cups (1/4-inch dice) honeydew melon
2 tablespoons fresh lemon juice

2 tablespoons chopped fresh cilantro leaves
1/4 teaspoon salt

In medium bowl, stir cantaloupe, honeydew, lemon juice, cilantro, and salt until mixed. Set aside.

Each 1/4 cup: About 15 calories, 0g protein, 4g carbohydrate, 0g total fat (0g saturated), 40mg sodium.

Peach Salsa

Serve with Spiced Grilled Turkey Breast (page 88) or grilled pork chops.

PREP: 15 MINUTES   MAKES ABOUT 4 CUPS

3 pounds ripe peaches, peeled, pitted, and cut into 1/2-inch cubes
1 green onion, finely chopped
2 tablespoons fresh lime juice
1 small hot red pepper such as cayenne, seeded and minced
1/2 teaspoon salt

In medium bowl, stir peaches, green onion, lime juice, hot pepper, and salt until mixed.

Each 1/4 cup: About 30 calories, 1g protein, 7g carbohydrate, 0g total fat (0g saturated), 75mg sodium.

Asian Salsa

This simple and refreshing salsa, with crisp cucumbers and fragrant mint, goes well with grilled chicken of any kind.

PREP: 15 MINUTES   MAKES ABOUT 3 1/2 CUPS

4 medium Kirby cucumbers (about 4 ounces each), unpeeled and each cut lengthwise into quarters then crosswise into 1/4-inch-thick pieces
1 medium carrot, peeled and grated
1 cup loosely packed fresh mint leaves, chopped
1/4 cup seasoned rice vinegar

In medium bowl, place cucumbers, carrot, mint, and rice vinegar; toss to combine. If not serving right away, cover and refrigerate up to 1 day.

Each 1/4 cup: About 15 calories, 0g protein, 3g carbohydrate, 0g total fat (0g saturated), 135mg sodium.

Southwest Corn Salsa

Toss fresh summer corn kernels with bold southwestern flavors and a splash of lime for a delicious accompaniment to grilled chicken.

PREP: 15 MINUTES   MAKES ABOUT 4 CUPS

2 limes
4 cups fresh corn kernels (cut from about 8 ears)
1/3 cup finely chopped red pepper
1 jalapeño chile, seeded and minced
1 green onion, thinly sliced

1/2 cup loosely packed fresh cilantro leaves, chopped
1/2 teaspoon salt
1/8 teaspoon coarsely ground black pepper
1/8 teaspoon ground cumin

From limes, grate 1/2 teaspoon peel and squeeze 3 tablespoons juice; place in medium bowl. Add corn, red pepper, jalapeño, green onion, cilantro, salt, pepper, and cumin; toss to combine. If not serving right away, cover and refrigerate up to 1 day.

Each 1/4 cup: About 35 calories, 1g protein, 8g carbohydrate, 0g total fat (0g saturated), 8mg cholesterol, 80mg sodium.

Tomato and Lemon Salsa

With flavors reminiscent of the Mediterranean, this salty, tangy condiment will heighten the taste of not only simple grilled chicken but also grilled lamb, beef, and pork.

PREP: 20 MINUTES   MAKES ABOUT 4 CUPS

1 medium lemon
3 medium tomatoes (about 1 pound), cut into 1/4-inch pieces
1 cup loosely packed fresh basil leaves, chopped

1/2 cup Kalamata olives, pitted and coarsely chopped

1. From lemon, grate $1/2$ teaspoon peel. Cut lemon in half; wrap and refrigerate 1 half lemon for another use. From remaining half lemon, cut off peel and white pith; remove segments from membranes and discard pits. Coarsely chop segments.

2. In medium bowl, place lemon peel, chopped lemon with any juice, tomatoes, basil, and olives; toss to combine. If not serving right away, cover and refrigerate up to 1 day.

Each $1/4$ cup: About 15 calories, 0g protein, 2g carbohydrate, 1g total fat (0g saturated), 0mg cholesterol, 45mg sodium.

Mango and Red Pepper Salsa

A colorful condiment that balances sweet mango with hot jalapeño.

PREP: 20 MINUTES   MAKES ABOUT 4 CUPS

2 ripe mangoes, peeled, pitted and cut into 1/4-inch pieces

1/2 small red pepper, cut into 1/4-inch pieces (about 1/2 cup)

1/2 English (seedless) cucumber, unpeeled and cut into 1/4-inch pieces

1 jalapeño chile, seeded and minced

3 tablespoons fresh lime juice

1/4 teaspoon salt

1/8 teaspoon coarsely ground black pepper

In large bowl, place mangoes, red pepper, cucumber, jalapeño, lime juice, salt, and pepper; toss to combine. If not serving right away, cover and refrigerate up to 1 day.

Each 1/4 cup: About 25 calories, 0g protein, 7g carbohydrate, 0g total fat (0g saturated), 0mg cholesterol, 50mg sodium.

Horseradish Salsa

For a peppier salsa, add more horseradish.

PREP: 15 MINUTES   MAKES 2 CUPS

3 ripe medium tomatoes (about
  1 pound), cut into 1/2-inch pieces
1 cup loosely packed fresh parsley
  leaves, chopped
1/2 small red onion, minced

2 tablespoons bottled white
  horseradish
1 tablespoon balsamic vinegar
1 tablespoon olive oil
1/2 teaspoon salt

In medium bowl, place tomatoes, parsley, red onion, horseradish, vinegar, oil, and salt; toss to combine. Cover and refrigerate until serving time.

Each 1/4 cup: About 35 calories, 1g protein, 4g carbohydrate, 2g total fat (0g saturated), 0mg cholesterol, 180mg sodium.

Fire-Roasted Tomato Salsa

Serve this wonderfully smoky, spicy dip on grilled fish or meat or with tortilla chips.

PREP: 15 MINUTES   GRILL: ABOUT 8 MINUTES   MAKES ABOUT 3 CUPS

Grilled Plum Tomatoes (opposite)
1 large jalapeño chile
1/4 cup minced red onion
1/3 cup chopped fresh cilantro

1/4 cup fresh lime juice
3/4 teaspoon salt
tortilla chips

1. Prepare Grilled Plum Tomatoes as directed.

2. While tomatoes are grilling, place whole jalapeño on same rack and grill over medium-high heat, turning occasionally, until skin is charred and blistered, about 8 minutes. Transfer jalapeño to cutting board; set aside until cool enough to handle.

3. Remove stem, skin, and seeds from jalapeño; discard. Finely chop jalapeño. Chop tomatoes.

4. In large bowl, combine jalapeño, tomatoes with their juices, onion, cilantro, lime juice, and salt. If not serving right away, cover and refrigerate up to 3 hours. Serve with tortilla chips.

Each 1/4 cup: About 40 calories, 1g protein, 4g carbohydrate, 3g total fat (0g saturated), 0mg cholesterol, 250mg sodium.

Grilled Plum Tomatoes

Be sure to use plum tomatoes. They are firm with low moisture content and hold up well when grilled.

PREP: 10 MINUTES   GRILL: ABOUT 8 MINUTES
MAKES 8 ACCOMPANIMENT SERVINGS

2 pounds plum tomatoes (about 8 large), cored and each cut lengthwise in half

2 tablespoons olive oil
1/2 teaspoon salt
1/4 teaspoon ground black pepper

1. Prepare outdoor grill for covered direct grilling over medium-high heat.
2. In large bowl, toss tomatoes with oil, salt, and pepper.
3. Place tomatoes on hot grill rack over medium-high heat. Cover grill and cook tomatoes, turning once, until they begin to char and soften, 8 to 10 minutes.

Each serving: About 50 calories, 1g protein, 5g carbohydrate, 4g total fat (1g saturated), 0mg cholesterol, 155mg sodium.

Creamy Peanut Dipping Sauce

Serve this sauce with our Mixed Grill with Asian Flavors (page 140), or use it as a dressing for a crunchy slaw.

PREP: 20 MINUTES PLUS STANDING
MAKES ABOUT 2 1/2 CUPS

3/4 cup creamy peanut butter
1/4 cup boiling water
3/4 cup well-stirred unsweetened
  light coconut milk (not cream of
  coconut)
1/2 cup packed fresh cilantro leaves,
  chopped

2 tablespoons packed brown sugar
2 tablespoons soy sauce
5 teaspoons seasoned rice vinegar
1/2 teaspoon crushed red pepper
1 small garlic clove, crushed with
  garlic press

In medium bowl, with wire whisk, mix peanut butter and boiling water until blended. Stir in coconut milk, cilantro, brown sugar, soy sauce, vinegar, crushed red pepper, and garlic until combined. Refrigerate sauce until ready to serve. Let stand at room temperature 30 minutes before serving to allow flavors to develop.

Each tablespoon: About 40 calories, 1g protein, 2g carbohydrate, 3g total fat (1g saturated), 0mg cholesterol, 100mg sodium.

TIP: For quick Asian Noodles toss sauce with 12 ounces cooked spaghetti or linguine. Top with 1 layer seedless cucumber that's been peeled and cut into matchstick strips. Serve at room temperature or chilled.

Vietnamese Dipping Sauce

A must at every Vietnamese table, no matter what is served. Use this piquant condiment for dipping meat, seafood, and vegetables, and for drizzling over rice.

PREP: ABOUT 12 MINUTES PLUS STANDING   MAKES ABOUT 1 CUP

1 jalapeño chile
3 tablespoons sugar
1 garlic clove, sliced
5 tablespoons Asian fish sauce
   (*nuoc nam*)

1 1/2 tablespoons fresh lime juice
2/3 cup warm water

1. Cut jalapeño crosswise into thin rings; discard seeds, if you like. Set aside one-third of rings for garnish. Place sugar, garlic, and remaining jalapeño in mortar; with pestle, pound into a coarse paste. (If you don't have a mortar, just mash to a paste with side of chef's knife.)

2. Transfer paste to small bowl; stir in fish sauce, lime juice, and warm water until blended. Add jalapeño rings. Set aside for 10 minutes before serving. If not using right away, cover and refrigerate up to 2 weeks.

Each tablespoon: About 15 calories, 1g protein, 3g carbohydrate, 4g total fat (0g saturated), 0mg cholesterol, 215mg sodium.

Soy Marinade

This wonderful combination of Asian flavors turns chicken or pork into a scrumptious supper with no muss, no fuss. Simply let the meat marinate at least 1 hour and as long as 4 hours, then grill.

PREP: 10 MINUTES   MAKES ABOUT 1 CUP

1/3 cup soy sauce
3 tablespoons seasoned rice vinegar
2 tablespoons packed brown sugar
2 tablespoons minced, peeled fresh ginger
1 tablespoon vegetable oil
2 garlic cloves, crushed with garlic press
2 green onions, thinly sliced
1/2 teaspoon Asian sesame oil
1/4 teaspoon crushed red pepper

In medium bowl, stir together soy sauce, vinegar, brown sugar, ginger, vegetable oil, garlic, green onions, sesame oil, and crushed red pepper. Use for chicken or pork.

Each tablespoon: About 30 calories, 1g protein, 4g carbohydrate, 1g total fat (0g saturated), 0mg cholesterol, 530mg sodium.

Cucumber Relish

Delicious with our Chicken and Beef Saté (page 64) or served alongside grilled fish.

PREP: 10 MINUTES   MAKES ABOUT 2 1/2 CUPS

4 medium Kirby cucumbers (about 4 ounces each), cut into 1/4-inch pieces

1/4 cup seasoned rice vinegar

2 tablespoons chopped red onion

1 tablespoon vegetable oil

1/4 teaspoon crushed red pepper

In medium bowl, with spoon, combine cucumber, vinegar, red onion, vegetable oil, and crushed red pepper. Cover and refrigerate until ready to serve.

Each 1/4 cup: about 25 calories, 0g protein, 3g carbohydrate, 1g total fat (0g saturated), 0mg cholesterol, 120mg sodium.

INDEX

Metric Equivalents

The recipes that appear in this cookbook use the standard United States method for measuring liquid and dry or solid ingredients (teaspoons, tablespoons, and cups). The information on this chart is provided to help cooks outside the U.S. successfully use these recipes. All equivalents are approximate.

METRIC EQUIVALENTS FOR DIFFERENT TYPES OF INGREDIENTS

A standard cup measure of a dry or solid ingredient will vary in weight depending on the type of ingredient. A standard cup of liquid is the same volume for any type of liquid. Use the following chart when converting standard cup measures to grams (weight) or milliliters (volume).

Standard Cup	Fine Powder (e.g. flour)	Grain (e.g. rice)	Granular (e.g. sugar)	Liquid Solids (e.g. butter)	Liquid (e.g. milk)
1	140 g	150 g	190 g	200 g	240 ml
3/4	105 g	113 g	143 g	150 g	180 ml
2/3	93 g	100 g	125 g	133 g	160 ml
1/2	70 g	75 g	95 g	100 g	120 ml
1/3	47 g	50 g	63 g	67 g	80 ml
1/4	35 g	38 g	48 g	50 g	60 ml
1/8	18 g	19 g	24 g	25 g	30 ml

USEFUL EQUIVALENTS FOR LIQUID INGREDIENTS BY VOLUME

1/4 tsp	=				1 ml
1/2 tsp	=				2 ml
1 tsp	=				5 ml
3 tsp	= 1 tbls	=	1/2 fl oz	=	15 ml
	2 tbls	= 1/8 cup	1 fl oz	=	30 ml
	4 tbls	= 1/4 cup	2 fl oz	=	60 ml
	5 1/3 tbls	= 1/3 cup	3 fl oz	=	80 ml
	8 tbls	= 1/2 cup	4 fl oz	=	120 ml
	10 2/3 tbls	= 2/3 cup	5 fl oz	=	160 ml
	12 tbls	= 3/4 cup	6 fl oz	=	180 ml
	16 tbls	= 1 cup	8 fl oz	=	240 ml
	1 pt	= 2 cups	16 fl oz	=	480 ml
	1 qt	= 4 cups	32 fl oz	=	960 ml
			33 fl oz	= 1000 ml	= 1 l

USEFUL EQUIVALENTS FOR DRY INGREDIENTS BY WEIGHT
(To convert ounces to grams, multiply the number of ounces by 30.)

1 oz	=	1/16 lb	=	30 g
4 oz	=	1/4 lb	=	120 g
8 oz	=	1/2 lb	=	240 g
12 oz	=	3/4 lb	=	360 g
16 oz	=	1 lb	=	480 g

USEFUL EQUIVALENTS FOR LENGTH
(To convert inches to centimeters, multiply the number of inches by 2.5.)

1 in	=			2.5 cm
6 in	=	1/2 ft	=	15 cm
12 in	=	1 ft	=	30 cm
36 in	=	3 ft	= 1 yd =	90 cm
40 in	=			100 cm = 1 m

USEFUL EQUIVALENTS FOR COOKING/OVEN TEMPERATURES

	Fahrenheit	Celsius	Gas Mark
Freeze Water	32° F	0° C	
Room Temperature	68° F	20° C	
Boil Water	212° F	100° C	
Bake	325° F	160° C	3
	350° F	180° C	4
	375° F	190° C	5
	400° F	200° C	6
	425° F	220° C	7
	450° F	230° C	8
Broil			Grill